Frantz Fanon

Titles in the series Critical Lives present the work of leading cultural figures of the modern period. Each book explores the life of the artist, writer, philosopher or architect in question and relates it to their major works.

In the same series

Frantz Fanon

James S. Williams

REAKTION BOOKS

Published by Reaktion Books Ltd
Unit 32, Waterside
44–48, Wharf Road
London N1 7UX, UK

www.reaktionbooks.co.uk

First published 2023
Copyright © James S. Williams 2023

Printed and bound in Great Britain by TJ Books Ltd, Padstow, Cornwall

A catalogue record for this book is available from the British Library

ISBN 978 1 78914 831 2

Contents

Abbreviations

The following abbreviations refer to works by Fanon:

AF   *Frantz Fanon: Alienation and Freedom*, ed. Jean Khalfa
and Robert J. C. Young (2018)

AV   *L'An v de la révolution algérienne* (1959) / *A Dying Colonialism* (ADC)

DT   *Les Damnés de la terre* (1961) / *The Wretched of the Earth* (WE)

PN   *Peau noire, masques blancs* (1952) / *Black Skin, White Masks* (BS)

PRA   *Pour la révolution africaine* (1964) / *Toward the African Revolution* (TAR)

Other abbreviations used:

ALN   Armée de Libération Nationale

CNRA   Conseil National de la Révolution Algérienne

FLN   Front de Libération Nationale

GPRA   Gouvernement Provisoire de la République Algérienne

MNA   Mouvement National Algérien

OAS   Organisation Armée Secrète

Introduction: Fanon: Doctor, Writer, Revolutionary

By any measure, what Frantz Omar Fanon (1925–1961) achieved during his brief life was extraordinary. By the time of his death from leukaemia aged 36 in an American hospital and his subsequent burial in Algeria, this native of the former French colony of Martinique had been a soldier in the Second World War decorated for his bravery, a political militant in North Africa during the Algerian War of Independence (1954–62), a practising psychiatrist who developed a pioneering form of ethnopsychiatry, a well-regarded author of scientific articles, a groundbreaking political essayist and theorist, a teacher, ambassador and journalist, and a major pan-Africanist and internationalist. Fanon was a phenomenon: a new model of engaged intellectual who sought to connect absolutely with a people and nation on multiple fronts; an outlaw of Europe who became one of the most influential revolutionary thinkers of anti-colonialism; and an avatar and beacon of postcolonialism *avant la lettre*.

Fanon's lasting reputation rests on his writings of political theory and philosophy. This relatively modest number of books, essays and occasional pieces, written over barely a decade, constitute a far-reaching critique of the last days of French imperialism and offer dazzlingly original and radical perspectives on the colonial ideology of race and identity and its Manichean structure of racial segregration. Drawing directly on his own experience of anti-Black racism and dehumanization, *Peau noire, masques blancs* (1952; *Black Skin, White Masks*) revealed for the first time the stark reality of the psychic and subjective mechanisms of the colonial relation whereby the Black colonized interiorize the drives, myths and instincts projected on them by the White colonizers. Fanon understood acutely the originary violence of racialization and the terrible mental damage it inflicted on native peoples, who are imprisoned by the settler's gaze in a 'zone of nonbeing' and vainly searching for recognition. Armed with these foundational insights, Fanon undertook to decolonize the Black (and White) mind and to free human consciousness through a dialectics of emancipation. *L'An v de la révolution algérienne* (1959) (translated into English as *A Dying Colonialism*) provided a detailed study of the unprecedented mutations in society and national consciousness that were emerging in Algeria owing to the people's active rejection of French colonial oppression. He would later argue in the work for which he is best known, *Les Damnés de la terre* (The Wretched of the Earth), published in 1961, that decolonization and the freedom of authentic existence can be achieved only by destroying colonial structures through 'pure' violence, since this also destroys the alienated self that colonial rule has planted in the mind of the native. He advocated armed resistance, although he never promoted terrorism as such (equally, he never condemned it).

Fanon remains such a pivotal and compelling figure not only because he appeared to bridge so effortlessly the worlds of science and politics, as both practitioner and theorist, in his ceaseless effort to show the enormity of colonial injustice and the lived pathologies of everyday life under colonial rule, but also because he himself underwent profound transformations in an endlessly renewed attempt to transcend the psychological condition imposed upon him. Born Black in an 'old' French colony where he was raised Christian and believed himself to be both French and 'White', he later renounced his Martinican identity. In this momentous severing of ties, Fanon was the first to break the chain between Black Martinicans and France. He would eventually aspire to be Algerian, changing his name to Omar Ibrahim Fanon (although he spoke virtually no Arabic) and identifying completely with the nationalist cause, even to the point of consenting to die for Algeria. He ultimately conceived of himself as belonging to a future United

States of Africa where the frontiers of skin and cultural prejudice no longer prevailed – a New Man born out of the ashes of colonial alienation and redeemed in a reconstituted, post-racial world.

The facts of Fanon's intensively lived life and career and his agonizing personal path towards transcendence over alienation have often been lost in the telling of his story, which, with its epic and tragic dimensions, has become the stuff of myth: Fanon the reserved intellectual and ascetic who gave himself to a militant cause with fundamentalist fervour; Fanon the committed medic working clandestinely in war-torn Algeria; Fanon the warrior-diplomat making undercover trips to sub-Saharan Africa while dodging assassination attempts; Fanon the martyr battling heroically against a fatal disease to complete his final written declaration of love for the Algerian people; Fanon the agent of freedom who liberated people's minds; Fanon the apostle of mystical violence and avenging angel of the Third World. Seduced by Fanon's visionary power, dynamism and charisma, critics, activists, memoirists and hagiographers alike have tried to (re)claim him, often piously, such as the Martinican poet and playwright Daniel Boukman, who followed the path of Fanon to Algeria and who regards him as an 'exemplary' man. For Boukman, Fanon's extreme but never fanatical acts of humanism were in total accord with his trailblazing writings in a perfect matching of the life and the work.[1]

Yet just as Fanon's contestatory essays were elaborate, multilayered, porous works, so too was his restless life, which he lived as a daily challenge in his quest to achieve optimum clarity and efficiency, but in which certain tensions, contradictions and ambivalences remained opaque and intractable – a fact Fanon readily recognized. For someone so sociable and talkative, Fanon almost never spoke publicly about himself and did not encourage discussion of his private life. He never gave a public interview and did not keep a diary. Questions about his life were cut short with a terse 'irrelevant!' Moreover, with the odd exception, there are no recordings of him speaking, just a few fleeting, spectral newsreel images of his attendance at conferences in Africa during the late

1950s and early 1960s, his voice inaudible. The adult Fanon rarely talked about his childhood after he left Martinique for good in 1952, and all but excised it from his memory – a sign of his astonishing capacity to compartmentalize his life and of his daunting willpower, which enabled him to reject the burden of the past in order to focus always on the present and the future. Even when he did allude to his lived experiences in his writing, it was for strategic and rhetorical reasons or to make general statements about Antillean society and culture. Such moments always come with a warning: beware the universalizing use of the first person, for there is nothing ever casual or merely anecdotal about Fanon.

Fanon was regarded by many during his lifetime as a man of obscure and sombre secrets who knew far more than he would ever let on – a sign of his discretion and the fact that he trusted few people and seldom confided in anyone, although he was supported unconditionally by his wife, family and some lifelong friends. Following his death, his life has been pieced together largely from the recollections of others. As his elder brother Joby lamented, Fanon has become a concatenation of legends constructed by those anxious to fill in the biographical blanks and retrieve his lost authentic voice by positing causes and effects, often based on misinformation. For instance, they suggested that as a child Fanon suffered terribly for perceiving his skin to be darker than that of his other siblings (it was not), or that as an adolescent he was a pupil of the Martinican poet Aimé Césaire (he was not) – as if Fanon could only have become 'Fanon' if he had suffered some major childhood trauma or encountered a fellow genius during his formative years to mark him out as exceptional.[2] Fanon remains to this day what Stuart Hall has called simply an 'enigma'.[3]

Perplexed by Fanon's uncertain, aleatory status (was he Martinican and/or French and/or Algerian, or 'just' Black?), some critics have also wished to pathologize him on account of his apparently futile and contradictory search for identity (the early Fanon trying to prove at all costs that he was French, the later Fanon trying to prove that he wasn't) while moving through global sites of trauma (the battlefields of European war, the asylums of France and North Africa, the arenas of armed revolution in Algeria). A contemporary of Fanon who did not know him personally, the French Tunisian writer Albert Memmi, famously summed up his extreme swerves in identity as a series of failures – proof of a doomed, 'impossible life' because Fanon never came to terms with his Martinican identity and thus never returned home to himself. For Memmi, Fanon's commitment to Algeria was a form of compensation for his disappointment with his homeland, and his identification with the Algerian nation a psychological substitute for 'an unattainable identification with Martinique'.[4] Yet Fanon's search to belong was less a wish for the security of home than an all-consuming desire to integrate himself within a society in transition. There are, of course, enormous dangers when one defines oneself so utterly in terms of a people and a nation, and when personal identity becomes more a matter of forging a new – as yet unknown – collective identity. Fanon dared in addition to decline all fixed settings of identity, which in his opinion entailed neurosis and fragmentation. If his primary focus was the embodied racial subject, his underlying aim was the deconstruction of all assigned identities based on essentializing perceptions of the Other. With such a revolutionary move, Fanon proposed every personal act as another step in a perpetual creation of selfhood and (self-) identity, with no one final destination or *telos*.

If one accepts that Fanon was a man who prioritized the process of *becoming* over that of being, one can better grasp how he could be simultaneously a practising doctor, a writer and a militant. Refusing to observe traditional disciplinary divisions, he worked at the intersection of psychiatry, psychoanalysis, anthropology and philosophy when these fields were undergoing major changes in Europe in the post-war period. His core revolutionary project of 'disalienation' was at once neurological, social, cultural and political, and this allowed him to be always on the move existentially rather than encased in identitarian structures premised on the notion of origin. It meant that he was intellectually a free agent and unaligned: Fanon did not belong to any one school of thought or political party or movement, although he was deeply influenced by Marx's ideas of revolution by the masses. He was a tireless innovator within existing paradigms and frameworks such as institutional psychiatry, Sartrean dialectics and revolutionary praxis. Such mobility is what makes Fanon so potent today: moving boldly and freely across multiple fields and domains, he was continually searching for more affirmative, revolutionary rhythms and convergences to counter the morbid narcissism and reification of colonialism and what he saw as the increasing petrification of European bourgeois society. Yet in whatever area he was operating, his primary approach was reparative, in that he endeavoured to understand better the symptoms of a condition and establish the correct diagnosis in the hope of finding a resolution or cure.

Fanon embraced life passionately, with boundless energy, an irrepressible enthusiasm for adventure and an overwhelming zeal and ambition. He was not one for half-measures or compromises: it was always all or nothing. An indefatigable workaholic who never took time off and who defined himself by his public acts, including writing (Fanon spoke and wrote expressly for an audience), he lived in the immediacy of the present moment and was invariably in combat mode, a man on a mission, living on his nerves and thriving on new challenges. As a doctor he was hard-wired to do whatever it took to achieve the desired result as swiftly and expediently as possible. Yet Fanon was also a rolling set of paradoxes. To take a prime example: for someone so confident and steadfast in his pursuits, so sure of his razor-sharp intellect and acumen, so brimming in self-belief regarding his faculties and powers of seduction (he openly acknowledged his egocentrism), he was not at ease in his own skin and could appear defensive in his nervous loquacity. He accounted for this in terms of his cultural background, since from the day he was born he had had to counter the 'crushing objecthood' (*PN* 88, *BS* 109) projected onto him of the mythological Negro of cosmopolitan French fantasies. He was forever on his guard. In the eyes of many who knew him, including his first publisher, Francis Jeanson, and the Martinican writer Édouard Glissant, he was 'écorché vif' ('hypersensitive') (literally, 'skinned alive'). Fanon's inner emotions ran deep, and he was not shy about venting feelings of indignation, hurt or humiliation at an opportune moment. As some of his writings attest and his brother Joby confirmed, while he exuded pure affirmation he was also permanently haunted by death.[5] Yet at the same time Fanon could not bear weakness in himself or others and had an instinctive aversion to displays of sentiment and vulnerability. Always impeccably dressed, he was a study in self-control and adopted a stern, laconic air in public, to the point of seeming detached and aloof. However, he was also blessed with a genuine (often grim) sense of humour and could, in the right company, don an open-neck shirt and dance and drink like the best of them.

In short, Fanon was a fascinatingly complex character of multiple guises and contradictory selves, like the dramatis personae in a continuous performance of shifting modes and fluctuating modalities. A born performer and raconteur, he possessed a versatility that was evident in the elastic features of his face, which could morph in public like that of a mime artist depending on the people he was with or the stories he was relating. On the cover of the Penguin edition of *Peau noire* he is pictured dramatically, with growling, heavy lips, a deep, furrowed forehead, blazing eyes and a slash mark on his left cheek. He never actively courted the limelight and had little time for photo ops or conference protocol, but when he chose to be visible he revelled in the attention and could transfix an audience. Photographs and frames of film capture him in full flow, striking a pose: the head doctor marching forwards with a train of assistants; the conference delegate squaring up to an audience; the globetrotting diplomat embarking and disembarking; the proud father pushing his young son in a pram in Tunis. Such lability helps explain why the material body and skin are of such theoretical interest to Fanon, who understood phenomenologically that race was inscribed viscerally in the skin. It accounts also for his detailed descriptions of the body and psyche under colonial stress, and why he was constantly searching for a new political skin: 'We must turn over a new leaf [*faire peau neuve*], we must work out new concepts,' he urges in *Les Damnés* (*DT* 305, *WE* 255).

Fanon in action at the Charles-Nicolle hospital, Tunis, during the late 1950s.

To insist on Fanon's performativity and myriad selves, and that at every level in his life and work identity remains in transit, is to appreciate the high stakes of his mobile, multifarious thought and writings. A consummate stylist, he approached each new text as a fresh experiment, an original configuration of political, philosophical and psychiatric lines of inquiry, at once analytical and creative, and tailored for a particular audience or reader whom he obliged to enter into a critical relation, even confrontation. We witness a self-styled man of reason trained in control, engaging intimately with emotions and affect (the agitations of his patients; the violent highs of literature that so attracted him; the churning desires for revolution), resulting in a form of writing that is both intellectual and sensual, the precise balance conditional on the context. On certain occasions Fanon also employs literary form as a means of emotional release, to alleviate his own perturbations and upset or else sustain passing moments of joy. There are, in fact, different tempos and rhythms in Fanon's writing, for while he was equally rigorous and creative in his empirically based clinical work and his more philosophical critical writings, and in each case attuned to the ethical implications of his speculations, the patient, methodical Fanon collaborating with his medical team contrasts greatly with the animated, at times breathless, Fanon intervening solo in theoretical debates or responding to unfolding political events. The distinction here is also between Fanon the sober diagnostician, carefully preparing a medical treatment plan, and Fanon the fast and furious idealist using his social diagnoses as a springboard for imagining radical change, with the attendant risk of incompletion – a risk Fanon fully assumed. There are moments when the clarity of his message becomes shaded by ambiguity and inconsistency, heightened by a messianic streak that runs throughout the corpus – the result of a liberatory consciousness emerging in the present of writing and exposed to the contingencies of the body and sensation. For these reasons Fanon's written work dramatizes his permanent, sometimes anguished, drive towards self-creation and self-invention without offering a final solution or interpretation.

Resisting, therefore, the reductive urge to conflate the defining paradoxes of Fanon the man with the rich complexities of his work and subsume them into a seamless, totalizing whole ('Fanon'), I wish to keep them in dynamic tension and parallel. The astonishing polyvalency of Fanon's writings and thought can best be approached by foregrounding the multiple flows and counterflows of his entangled life as he travelled interminably back and forth through different time zones and national territories. Each new crossing was a potential turning point in his life and career and a new stage in his (self-)transformation that reflected the mutations in his thinking and inspired the decisive leaps and breaks, diversions and deviations in his clinical, political and literary practice. Encountering Fanon afresh requires also bringing back into the frame the influential female elements in his life who have often been left out of the official Fanon story: his mother; his close medical colleague and friend (and future biographer) in North Africa, Alice Cherki; and, above all, his French wife, Josie, who outlived him by almost three decades and who has usually been cast as a side note, important only for forming with Fanon an ideal multiracial couple and producing an heir. According to this version, Josie supplied merely the necessary stability for Fanon to be 'Fanon', including her dutiful function as his private secretary, taking down the great man's words as he dictated and serving as a model for the mainly female assistants who transcribed and typed up his work. Yet Josie was a fully active and present force in Fanon's life, his muse and comrade who shared his immediate allegiance to Algeria, breaking away from France just as he did and committing wholly to the Algerian cause. She understood that almost everything Fanon wrote was based in some way on personal experience and not some abstract theory. However, in another telling instance of how Fanon kept his personal and public life determinedly separate, there are no extant public photographs of Frantz and Josie together.

This critical biography charts and celebrates Fanon's exemplary commitment to movement and change by exploring his life and work together as part of a fluid and necessarily incomplete organic process of consciousness – an evolving, multi-textured self in continual motion. I wish to retain the rush of Fanon's performative energy: the excitement of his openness to uncertainty, his investment in self-renewal and self-reinvention, and his loyalty to the event to come. As he put it in *Peau noire*, the human being 'is motion toward the world' (*PN* 33, *BS* 41), adding: 'In the world through which I travel, I am endlessly creating myself . . . And it is by going beyond the historical, instrumental hypothesis that I will initiate my cycle of freedom' (*PN* 186–7, *BS* 229–31). By tracking Fanon's life and writing together in this way and taking full account of newly available primary material,[6] we will be able to discern the profound continuities in his multi-corpus but also its faultlines and tensions, when Fanon the writer rubs up against Fanon the psychiatrist and Fanon the political activist in the often diverging relations between theory and practice. We shall also see how Fanon's indomitable voluntarism and belief in the absolute power of the will, together with his wish to micromanage the present, were beset by limitations that complicate any simple reading of his utopian thought, notably regarding violence and sexuality. Fanon's lifelong search for a genuinely progressive humanism may ultimately lack a final clear definition, but the urgency and profusion of his multiple lives and unique, still-refulgent oeuvre inspire what now follows.

1

More French than French: Boyhood on a Colonial Island

The tropical, mountainous island of Martinique, part of the French Antilles in the eastern Caribbean Sea, has a documented history stretching back to the sixteenth century when Christopher Columbus arrived there in 1502. However, it was not until 1635, when the French trader Pierre Bélain d'Esnambuc landed in the harbour of Saint-Pierre, that the island became a colonial possession. With its fertile volcanic soil, Martinique was quickly turned into a French slave colony, with people transported from West Africa during the initial period of sugar cane cultivation followed by that of coffee in the 1720s. The original Carib population gradually disappeared due to expulsion by the French or because of disease. Slavery was briefly abolished in 1794 in the wake of the French Revolution but fully ended only in 1848, when the French journalist and politician Victor Schoelcher decreed that it be terminated in the name of assimilation. The island maintained a tightly stratified social system: at the top stood a small group of around a thousand white-skinned descendants of the early European settlers called *békés* – a close-knit, endogamous community who controlled three-fourths of the land. Below them came a burgeoning middle class composed predominantly of people of mixed race, known as mulattoes or *mulâtres*. At the bottom lay the Black labouring class. The overall population amounted to around 300,000 in the early years of the twentieth century.

It was into this bleak and rigid colonial system of White supremacism and capitalism that Frantz Marguerite Victor Fanon was born on 20 July 1925, the fifth of eight children.[1] His was a

A view of Fort-de-France, November 1925.

fairly typical Black bourgeois Martinican family. They lived in the
bourg of Fort-de-France, which had recently become the island's
new capital after Saint-Pierre and its 30,000 inhabitants were
destroyed by the volcanic explosion of Mont Pelée in 1902. Fanon's
father, Félix Casimir, a customs inspector, was the mixed-race
son of a freed Black slave and an East Indian woman. His mother,
Éléonore Félicia Médélice, a haberdasher, was of mixed ancestry,
with a French background on her mother's side, her Alsatian roots
no doubt accounting for the name chosen for her third son, Frantz.
The fact that, in the island's intricate racial scheme of *métissage*,
Éléonore was a *mulâtresse* conferred on her a sense of hierarchy:
this was a society that obsessively classified people according to
skin pigment colour and where the factor of illegitimacy was of
less importance than the ethnic quotient. Frantz's two uncles were
both professionals: Édouard was a school teacher and Albert a
civil servant working for the Office des Eaux et Forêts. Like most
middle-class *mulâtres*, the family had little contact with the *békés*
(whether White businessmen or the island's plantocracy), yet they

aspired to full assimilation and sought to emulate the manners and language of the Whites by speaking impeccable French, a sign of metropolitan status. The Fanons were, in fact, a model of upward social mobility, able to afford servants (a prized symbol of class) as well as music lessons for the girls. The mother's excellent financial sense allowed them to build, in the nearby village of Redoute, a second house for weekends with an impressive garden. However, an abiding part of the family's collective memory remained that of a *béké* on horseback with a whip in hand. Joby, Frantz's elder brother by two years, talked of their grandfather being driven off his rented plot of land for cocoa farming in this brutal fashion.[2]

In the image of compartmentalized Martinican society, Fort-de-France was mapped according to a hierarchy of areas and narrow streets. The small but comfortable family home (also Éléonore's place of business) was situated at 33 rue de la République, one of the major thoroughfares in the centre and close to the main civic buildings, including the town hall. Immediately north of the centre was Terres-Sainville, where the other, poorer, Black population

Rue Antoine Siger in central Fort-de-France, *c.* 1930.

lived. Frantz and his siblings played on the nearby Parc de la Savane, a dusty, unevenly paved open space 200 metres (650 ft) long and populated by worm-eaten tamarind trees. At one end, in front of the Bibliothèque Schoelcher, an ornate yet flea-ridden public library built in 1887, stood a statue of the island native Joséphine de Beauharnais, the daughter of a wealthy colonial family who later became the first wife of Napoléon Bonaparte. The overall effect was of a slightly dilapidated version of a French provincial city, with architecture falling just below the usual standards of Second Empire style. Fanon later wrote, directly citing Aimé Césaire, that the city, hemmed in by a cluster of steep hills, was stultifyingly flat and inert, dirty and stinking (*PN* 17, *BS* 21). It was also ridden with disease, including smallpox, tuberculosis and malaria, and the open gutters were like running sewers: since the city was at sea level, any rising tide would bring sewage directly back up the drains into the centre.

The internal dynamic of the Fanon family was conventionally Martinican and reflected the island's matrifocal society. Casimir, a diligent and discreet functionary, was a distant and uninvolved father but also a freethinker as well as a musician, dancer and all-round charmer, imparting to his children a sense of duty and educating them in tolerance and respect for the ideas of others – traits that had a lasting influence on Frantz. Éléonore was a 'strong-minded intellectual woman',[3] generous and mild-mannered, yet she was also a natural authority figure who imposed the law of the (often absent) father and instilled the Catholic faith in which she fervently believed. This religious background clearly informed Fanon's youth, however much he and his brothers tried to skip religious education on Thursdays, and it marked him deeply, establishing a wellspring of Christian ideas and motifs that he would instinctively draw on in his writing. Éléonore appears to have favoured her obedient daughters over her sons, to whom she was not overly affectionate or warm; Frantz, a sensitive child, she regarded as mainly a cheeky and restless troublemaker. Although acquiring from his parents the adult virtues of self-possession and self-restraint, including a propensity not to display emotion or 'sentimentality', Frantz was naturally outgoing and ebullient, playful and athletic.[4] They reasoned that he must have been exchanged at the hospital (he was the only child not born at home) to be so vivacious. He was discouraged from speaking Creole, the first language of almost all Martinicans but which was deemed a *patois* – somewhere between *petit-nègre* (pidgin French) and French. Middle-class mulatto mothers would scold their children caught speaking Creole with the word '*tibandes*', to indicate they were no better than the *petites bandes*, or gangs of Black children who worked in the sugar cane fields. Hence, while he spoke Creole with his friends, Frantz wrote in French. At home, Éléonore admonished him to 'stop acting like a n[****]r' whenever he wished to listen and dance to Creole music (*PN* 155, *BS* 191); for this reason Fanon always associated music and dance with freedom.

Like most young Foyolais, as the inhabitants of Fort-de-France were called (the town was originally named Fort-Royal), the young Fanon spent a good part of his days in the streets, where his innate tendency to assume the role of leader led him to captain a small group of children whom he called 'Les Joyeux Compagnons'. Of the four sons he was the most daring and irreverent, indulging in minor boyhood pranks and tricks and becoming ever more mischievous in early adolescence, sometimes getting into fights where he gave as good as he got. On one occasion, when he was physically assaulted by three boys from another family, he immediately fought back, even using a razor blade to defend himself. Along with his brothers he was considered a danger to the rue Blénac, just a few streets away from the family home, and even branded a dangerous vagabond. Together with Joby, to whom he was closest, he became part of a gang called 'La bande raide' that committed petty theft, even in their own mother's shop. At Redoute, meanwhile, the brothers enjoyed a wild sense of freedom when the parents were at work and only the servants were around. All this was permitted because the boys continued to do well at school and the trouble they caused was largely harmless.

There was, however, the occasional moment of genuine risk and danger, as when a childhood friend of Frantz's fourteen-year-old brother Félix, Kléber Gamess, visited the Fanon household with his father's revolver to impress the brothers. Unaware that the gun was loaded, Kléber fired it, injuring his index finger and nearly shooting Frantz, who immediately tore a sheet and wrapped Kléber's bloody finger, explaining to his mother that the noise was merely a toy backfiring. He then calmly escorted Kléber to hospital. To say that this incident marked the trajectory of the future physician and revolutionary – the Fanon who could remain cool and collected in volatile situations, the Fanon who ended up training guerrillas in an Algerian hospital basement – would be to overdetermine its significance. Yet the event is instructive of Fanon's inherent ability to keep a steady head and ensure an efficient and safe outcome. It also corresponded to the steadily growing impression of Frantz as a brave, intense individual with an acute sense of justice who always stood his ground. In the busy courtyard of the family home he was already taking a stand on matters and holding forth like a champion of the people.

The one potentially life-changing episode in Fanon's childhood was more psychological than physical, and its status remains ambiguous. It involves the recollection by his future colleague Alice Cherki of a memory Fanon once shared with her. He claimed that at the age of ten he was taken as a schoolboy to the Schoelcher monument in front of the Palais de Justice to render homage. He wondered why Schoelcher was a hero and what had happened before 1848, which was never talked about. Was this an instance of invented memory by the adult Fanon? Cherki acknowledges his fondness for fabulation yet concludes that it did not really matter if the memory was retrofitted since it clearly formed him. He now understood for the first time that what was being promoted by his elders was based on denial and a falsified account of history. After this, Fanon explained to her, although he continued to play sport and go to the cinema, nothing else was the same again – as if he had opened his eyes and ears for the first time.[5]

In truth, though, this event, even if accurate, was not a momentous turning point for Fanon while growing up, for he continued to believe unquestioningly that as a Martinican he was French and thus belonged to France's republican history,

The statue of Victor Schoelcher outside the Palais de Justice, Fort-de-France.

society and culture. He was indoctrinated in the French colonial system and its 'civilizing mission', which demanded assimilation: children were taught to celebrate the history of France and the glory of French culture while depreciating the (Black) African way of life. Hence Frantz thought of himself as a son of the French Revolution rather than of African heritage. The identification was absolute, and Fanon would later write that at school he had to listen to accounts of the savage Senegalese against whom he defined himself as an Antillean: 'Subjectively, intellectually, the Antillean [that is, the educated bourgeois Black] conducts himself like a white man' (*PN* 120, *BS* 148). Further: 'I am a white man. For unconsciously I distrust what is black in me, that is, the whole of my being'

(*PN* 154–5, *BS* 191). In the words of one biographer, education was 'an induction into linguistic and cultural schizophrenia'.[6] As the human rights analyst Rita Maran also argues, the colonized man, 'object of the civilizing mission', was never fully a man because his rights as a subject were posited but never fulfilled. It was a double bind: 'The colonized could not reach adulthood under colonialism, despite the fact that to make him into "man" was a key legitimizing doctrine of colonialism – its "educational" mission.'[7]

For Fanon, the source of the problem in Martinique was historical: in the 1848 emancipation, 'the White Master, *without conflict*, recognized the Negro slave' (*PN* 176, *BS* 217; original emphasis), a process that denied what he saw as the necessary healthy confrontation between master and slave (*PN* 178, *BS* 219). Antilleans had never defeated the old master by means of a life-or-death struggle, a crucial step towards mastery and self-being, for while they 'went from one way of life to another' they did not move 'from one life to another' (*PN* 178, *BS* 220). Gifted freedom by their former masters, they never truly liberated themselves. Put differently, rather than acting for themselves, they had been acted upon. For this reason, the Black Frenchman, although free physically and politically, remained bound psychologically and subjectively.

The seeds of Fanon's political self-consciousness and ultimate rejection of Martinique as a region lacking historicity and collective resistance were subconsciously sown during his boyhood. Only much later, however, would he come to understand the process of Frenchification as brainwashing and a device to turn the Afro-Martinican subject into a Frenchified 'object' in all aspects of life (culture, language, education, history, legacy). Only then, too, would he realize how profoundly alienating, racist and suffocating this experience was, and that within French society he would always be defined by his colour, whether as a Black student or a Black doctor. For now, growing up in a large, tight-knit and comfortable Black bubble, Frantz identified totally with the culture into which he had been instructed. He felt – *he was* – French. Moreover, with his mother being so immensely ambitious for her children, he was preoccupied like all his siblings by his future prospects. Five of the eight children would go on to university, a decision that required, after the *baccalauréat*, an obligatory, onerous move to France since there was no institution of higher education on the island. The opportunities for a Black graduate in the Antilles were limited to just a few professions: medicine, dentistry, pharmacy and, to a lesser extent, law. Joby would study law in Paris and work as a customs officer in Paris, Moroni (in the Comoros) and Strasbourg, while the youngest brother, Willy, would work for the Ministry of Education in Paris. Éléonore's daughters were similarly dutiful and driven and wished at all costs to avoid the fate of Black girls later portrayed by the Martinican writer Mayotte Capécia as dreaming of White husbands in order to secure social promotion.[8] Three of them would pursue a professional career and integrate smoothly into a married, middle-class, Martinican existence.

Being so inquisitive, intelligent and eager for knowledge, Frantz was a highly able student. He had exceptional verbal and visual recall, able to memorize instantly and recite whole verses of poetry, yet he was increasingly bored at his primary school, the École Perrinon. He did not fit the mould of a typical hard worker and was rarely seen studying, although he possessed a remarkable capacity to undertake work if required. He was – and always would be – ahead of his immediate entourage, and, as so often, he relied on his elder brother Joby's active support to leave Perrinon a year early by sitting the Certificat d'Études Primaires (CEP) independently as a *candidat libre*, to the chagrin of his teachers. After joining Joby to undertake *cours complémentaires* (additional secondary-level courses) at Terres-Sainville, he started to lose interest in *vagabondage*, dedicating more time to reading, especially fiction and poetry (he was top of his class in French). The three brothers joined football clubs (for Frantz it was the Club Colonial), and it was on the football field, where he played centre-forward, that Fanon first met Marcel Manville. The son of a Martinican socialist and three years older than Frantz, Manville would become a close and lifelong friend.

Fanon's boyhood was essentially uneventful and unexceptional for someone of his background, and he emerged from it robust, well-adjusted, and fundamentally unscathed by trauma or complexes.

He was healthy and gregarious and enjoyed the mutual respect and unconditional love of his family, in particular Joby and his closest sister, Gabrielle, three years his senior. What is perhaps most foundational about Fanon's experience of family unity and harmony – actively encouraged by his mother, who fostered a sense of loyalty that excluded anyone not a blood relative – is that it gave him an unwavering belief in his own abilities and the confidence always to speak his mind and expect to be heard. Only someone who has experienced such total union growing up could perhaps know what allegiance and solidarity really stood for and be prepared to fight tooth and nail to secure it. As he moved into adulthood, Fanon would always be searching for a new family of his own – an ideal form of kinship – to which he could similarly commit.

2

Fighting for the Republic:
From *Dissidence* to Combat

Fanon was fourteen years old when war broke out in Europe in
September 1939. Everything suddenly changed in Martinique.
If, as he later wrote, Antilleans had considered themselves relatively
happy (they voted, took part in carnival processions, drank
rum, danced to the *biguine*[1]), now they were gripped by panic
and fear that the island might be invaded by German forces.
Trenches were dug in the Parc de la Savane, which became a
new adventure playground for Frantz and his brothers before it
turned into a cesspool. On 15 September 1939, Admiral Georges
Robert was posted to Fort-de-France as High Commissioner for
the French West Indies and Commander in Chief of the West
Atlantic Fleet, arriving on the island on the cruiser *Jeanne d'Arc*.
Following the armistice of 1940 and the fall of France to the Vichy
administration, the USA imposed a blockade on Martinique
to prevent the transfer of gold deposits from local banks to
France. In response, Robert installed military hardware in the
harbour of Fort-de-France, including cruisers and a submarine
(the gold was stored at Fort Desaix, outside the capital). So
began what became known as 'Tan Robè', or 'Robert Time'.

    For the next three years, the French navy behaved like an
occupying force: 5,000 sailors (10,000 according to Fanon, who
knowingly exaggerated the number) descended on the city's
population of 45,000 for a prolonged vacation. They ran riot,
expropriating the bars, hotels and restaurants, and ordering
civilians around, sometimes brutally. Prices quickly spiralled
owing to the abundance of military money, and Martinicans

found they could no longer afford basic goods, creating near-famine conditions. There was no meat for the local population, and food rationing began. To survive required ingenuity and reliance on the emerging black market. By 1941 the colour lines were well established: cafés were now segregated (Black waiters served White customers), and sailors requisitioned women, even young girls, as prostitutes; if that didn't work, they raped them. A statute was introduced against the small number of Jews on the island, and the death penalty was declared for anyone who thought of joining the Free French forces outside Martinique. Even Fanon's father fell under suspicion as a Freemason and thus potential supporter of the secular Left, placing the family under further strain. While collective acts of social disobedience did occur, such as refusing to sing the Marseillaise, setting fire to fields of crops or listening clandestinely to the BBC broadcast from the neighbouring islands of Dominica and Saint Kitts (at the time British colonies), the indigenous Black population was almost totally subjugated. Supported by the *béké* families who controlled almost all the land and commodities in Martinique, Robert had effectively established a military dictatorship. A personality cult even sprung up around him as 'our guide', as if he were Marshal Pétain himself in his all-white uniform.

Like all Black Martinicans, Fanon resented and hated Robert's racist, boorish and looting sailors. It was his first direct encounter with overt French racism and it shocked him: these were fellow French nationals who perceived him indiscriminately as *just another Negro.* The humiliation of finding himself instantly turned into the menial, worthless object of a racist White gaze was shattering. Yet the baseness of Robert's administration and sailors did not lead Fanon to a more general soul-searching about his French identity, nor did he link racism with colonial realities, for he clung to a clear distinction between 'real Frenchmen' and the racist 'false French' of Robert Time, whom he identified with the Germans who used Martinique to refuel their U-boats during the Battle of the Caribbean. He also kept himself busy: he and Joby worked together in the backstreets to recover money unpaid by their mother's clients.

Of course, Fanon still had to continue his schooling. Initially Éléonore sent Frantz and Joby to stay with their uncle Édouard, out of harm's way in the small town of Le François, 23 kilometres (14 mi.) away on the other side of the island. Unlike Fanon's indulgent father, Édouard was a strict paternal figure who encouraged his new charges to work hard and study. He also possessed a large library and encouraged his nephews to read the French literary canon, in particular Balzac and Zola. Frantz was soon writing essays that impressed his uncle, who detected literary talent. Both brothers thrived and gained in maturity owing to their encounters with local farmers and factory workers who opened their eyes to larger, more material issues and helped them recognize their own privileged position as city dwellers of a certain social class. When the two eventually returned to Fort-de-France in late summer 1940 for the new school year, Joby enrolled as a weekly boarder at the one secondary school in Martinique, the Lycée Schoelcher, affordable only to the Black bourgeois elite, in order to prepare for the *baccalauréat*. Frantz, meanwhile, returned to school at Terres-Sainville. During the weekly periods of separation from Joby he would spend his time alone, reading the classics under the grand Byzantine dome of the Bibliothèque Schoelcher.

In January 1943 Fanon decided to prepare for the first part of the *baccalauréat* a year early. Joby assiduously helped his brother study set authors such as Rousseau and Racine (Fanon knew by heart whole passages from *Bérénice* and *Britannicus*), thereby ensuring his success in the first written exams in June. Then, in early July, while preparing for the autumn session of the exams, Frantz suddenly declared to Joby that he was going to join the Free French forces as one of a rising number of illegal *dissidents*. The movement of *dissidence* was not a resistance organization as such, since the island was not officially occupied, but it represented an explicit choice by Fanon not to submit to the Pétainist administration.

Beyond the pervasive racism and increasing hardship and degradation of Robert Time, a number of factors contributed to Fanon's precipitous decision, including the harassment his father was suffering and the ban on listening to the BBC. More crucially, he wanted, as he later put it, to be 'in the very heart of the problem' (*PN* 164, *BS* 203) – that is, in the theatre of war – in order to help protect 'true France'. The Comité Français de Libération Nationale, created in June 1943, had now made Algiers its capital from which to coordinate the liberation of France. Fired up by Charles de Gaulle's messages from London to save France, Fanon believed freedom to be indivisible: at once individual and national, French and Martinican. Robert's sailors had forced him to discover his colour and defend it; and, in the context of the Antilles, to be against the old White indigenous plantocracy was to be for French republican ideology, with its rallying call of liberty, equality, fraternity.

Yet Fanon's first stirrings of political revolt in the name of freedom were also, ironically, an act of rebellion against his own family. Joby flatly dismissed Frantz's idea as naive and 'delirious' (Fanon was, after all, still only seventeen), accusing him not for the first time of dreaming, which he vehemently refuted.[2] In this first major turning point in Fanon's life, and a defining act of his headstrong and tenacious character, he was unshakable and could not be reasoned with. He had decided: there was nothing more to discuss. At such impulsive moments, when he would go it alone if necessary and do whatever was needed to get the job done, Fanon was like someone possessed. His instinctual spirit of defiance, overriding the wishes of even those closest to him, is also what helped make him so individual and unique.

A little later in July, on the same day that family members gathered to celebrate the wedding of his eldest brother, Félix, at Le Morne-Rouge, Frantz became one of the estimated 4,500 Martinicans who embarked on the dangerous 48-kilometre (30 mi.) crossing over rough waters to Dominica. He first had to make his way alone to the little port of Le Prêcheur in the northwest of the island before hopping enthusiastically on a *gommier*, a Caribbean canoe. In order to pay for the passage, he had pilfered two fabric coupons from his father's cupboard that had been set aside for the suits for Félix's wedding (a theft Casimir never entirely forgave). Safely landed, he underwent military training by the British army.

His brave, noble adventure in the battle against Nazism and racism came to a swift and anticlimactic end, however, for the Robert regime in Martinique was now all but over. The effects of the U.S. blockade and the rise of support for de Gaulle throughout the French Empire, combined with local anti-Pétainist demonstrations (including a major protest on 24 June in Fort-de-France), had led the island's elite to make a shrewd decision: to switch loyalties from the Vichy government to its Gaullist opponents. Martinique finally joined the Free French campaign, and the Free French forces took over the island on Bastille Day, 14 July 1943. Admiral Robert capitulated to pressure and departed from Martinique. As for Fanon, after being repatriated he returned to school with an overwhelming sense of deflation and embarrassment.

In the last months of 1943, the situation in Martinique changed still further, with the creation of a 5th Bataillon de Marche des Antilles (known as the BMA5) under Lieutenant-Colonel Henri

That ship had sailed: Free French *dissidents* from Martinique and Guadeloupe on board USS *Albemarle*, 1 May 1943, taking them from Puerto Rico to the United States to be trained as soldiers.

Tourtet, a Gaullist who had played a key role in the popular uprising against Robert. Propelled by what Joby considered a mixture of obstinacy and 'morbid perseverance', Fanon now wished to join the battalion for the rest of the war. As he put it to Joby: 'Each time the dignity and freedom of man are in question, we are all concerned, Blacks, Whites, Yellows, and each time liberty is threatened in whatever place, I will engage.'[3] He was, of course, once more going against the advice of his family as well as of his teachers, who believed that the war was a settling of accounts between Whites, whereas the problem for Martinicans remained a struggle against all Whites for complete emancipation. They counselled a wait-and-see attitude. This was not Fanon's temperament: he was impatient for results and tended always towards frontline engagement. Now eighteen, he was promptly enrolled, although owing to a lack of resources the USS *Oregon* could not depart immediately for Europe. When the vessel did finally set sail without fanfare in the early hours of 12 March 1944, with a thousand Black volunteers on board, Fanon was accompanied by his close older friends Marcel Manville and Pierre Mosole, all equally intoxicated by patriotic fervour. Fanon's mother entrusted her son to Manville in the desperate hope that Frantz might somehow be managed and kept safe. Not a single *béké* was on board.

Fighting for Freedom: Take Two

USS *Oregon* arrived in Casablanca on 30 March 1944. Reassigned to the 15th Régiment de Tirailleurs Sénégalais, Fanon then headed on to various posts in Morocco, including by train inland to the El Hajeb camp near Meknès for basic training as an officer cadet. This was a hub of inter-ethnic tensions and miserable physical conditions: a world of fraternity without equality where everyone was categorized and segregated according to racial type. At the top of the strict hierarchy were the White Europeans. The West Indians, who wore a *calot* (or side cap) on their heads, were treated ambivalently as 'half-European' because they came from the old colonies. Below them were the North Africans and Arabs, while the lowest of the low were the West Africans, the *tirailleurs sénégalais*. The field brothel was reserved for Martinicans only. The gross unfairness of the colonial military system dealt a rude blow to Fanon's enthusiasm, a situation not helped by his acute boredom, and it triggered residual feelings of recalcitrance. He made no effort to be a good soldier and began to play up with Manville and Mosole, even committing petty offences to see which of them would earn the worst military record. Manuel, the Martinican captain, took careful note, writing of Fanon in his report: 'Average soldier . . . An intelligent pupil, but of difficult character and doubtful military spirit.'[4]

In late May, Fanon received a transfer order to the Algerian port of Béjaïa, where he completed his cadet training. The unit then made its way across Algeria to Oran, where the shock of seeing famished Arab children fight savagely for the bread thrown to them by soldiers left an indelible impression on him (*DT* 295, *WE* 248). From Oran he set out in late August across the Mediterranean on an American-flagged boat as part of the follow-on convoy of Operation Dragoon, the Allied invasion of southern France initiated on 15 August. He arrived on an invasion beach near St Tropez on 31 August, remarkably still together with Manville and Mosole. They were incorporated into the 6th regiment of the 9th Colonial Infantry Division, which had sustained heavy losses during the fierce fighting to retake Toulon. Fanon was tasked with, among other things, guarding the deserted house of the late French writer Paul Bourget near Hyères, in the Var. After undergoing a baptism by fire in the village of La Valette-du-Var outside Toulon, he then joined the mortar division for a series of battles against the retreating Germans between the Rhône valley and the Swiss border.

Yet as he advanced up through the Rhône region towards Grenoble, Fanon started for the first time to feel profoundly unsure about his identity: was he a Black Frenchman (in distinction to a *tirailleur sénégalais*) or an honorary White *toubab* (European)?[5] For during the autumn of 1944, Black soldiers serving in the 9th Colonial Infantry Division and First Free French Division were routinely replaced by White French soldiers and partisans for the campaign in the Vosges mountains. De Gaulle later justified this policy of '*blanchiment*' ('whitening') on the grounds that because Black soldiers could not tolerate cold, their health was as at risk during the winter months.[6] In addition to such familiar prejudices was the very real fact of inadequate kit: the American forces were unable to supply enough equipment for all the French citizens from liberated territories who had now enrolled in the French military. Yet while spared from going into the freezing, snow-ridden northern areas, many Black soldiers regarded this policy paradoxically as a denial of their opportunity for frontline glory. Fanon himself was one of those sent north, and of one thing he was absolutely certain: non-White soldiers were being sent into action first for surprise attacks and were now accounting for the majority of casualties.

On 15 November, in a high woodland area called the Bois des Grappes, near Montbéliard in the Doubs (part of a military operation named 'La Boucle du Doubs'), Fanon was wounded in the chest by shrapnel from a mortar round while replenishing ammunitions (an 81-mm mortar) under enemy bombardment. The commander's notebook describes his courage and composure in

Soldiers of the French Colonial Infantry holding a position near Besançon in northeast France during the military operation known as La Boucle du Doubs, winter of 1944.

performing his mission, which compelled the admiration of his comrades.[7] (Fanon later revealed to Joby that he was the only soldier who dared to volunteer – the others had refused to move.[8]) For his valour he would in time be awarded the Croix de Guerre with a bronze star, signed by Colonel Raoul Salan of the 6th Colonial Infantry Regiment. For now he was evacuated and hospitalized at Nantua, in the Ain, where he established a lasting friendship with a wartime 'godmother', or *marraine de guerre* – the term for the French institution of female volunteers who adopted a serving soldier and provided moral support by writing letters (in some cases they even helped materially). In January 1945 he went to convalesce in Paris, where he claimed to have a brief affair with a young French woman called Paule.[9] Then, after rejoining his unit in late February, he was posted on 7 March to Hyères, before heading back to the front to take part in the Battle of Alsace.

On 12 April, Fanon penned an extraordinary two-page letter to his family that he later referred to as a 'sort of testament' from an 'habitant d'outre-vie' (that is, someone no longer of this earth).[10] In it, he expressed his devastating realization that he had come to Europe under false pretences to defend 'an obsolete ideal' and 'false ideology'. '*I was wrong!*' (original emphasis), he howled.[11] Fanon was particularly embittered by the complacency of the local peasants, who displayed little respect for those fighting on their behalf. His sense of mortifying disappointment, couched in religious rhetoric, was exacerbated by his belief that he was doomed to die on the battlefield in an imminent dangerous mission: 'If I didn't return and you learned one day of my death facing the enemy, console yourselves but never say he died for the good cause. Say: God has recalled him.'[12] We glimpse here, at its starkest, Fanon's apocalyptic sense of death.

But that is not all: addressing each family member in turn, and in characteristically direct and clinical fashion, Fanon first praised his mother's strength and commitment to her children ('Maman: it's here that I've truly seen what you represented for us') before launching into a no-holds-barred rebuke of his father's weakness. 'Papa, you really have failed at times in your duty as a father,' he declared, adding contemptuously: 'Look at yourself, see the years that have passed, bare your soul, have the courage to say: I deserted.'[13] With disconcerting candour and aggression he exhorted his father to give back a hundredth of what his mother had achieved in order to restore the 'equilibrium of the family', suggesting in what would become a familiar refrain that action (in this case an act of repentance) was meaningful only if conducted for the common good. The fact that Fanon framed his strictures as 'the reproaches of someone living in life's beyond' did little to justify them in the eyes of his mother, although it appears Casimir took the attack more philosophically.[14]

This first major personal written statement by Fanon – a stunning reversal of his fervid patriotism for France – exemplifies his ability to distil a stream of cascading emotions in a literary form (here, a letter from the front) and punctiliously dissect a series of discrete elements (the motherland of France, his mother, his father, the family). Yet it also reveals that, despite everything, Fanon's natural reflex was never to give up but to persevere, through sheer grit and determination, until he had accomplished his duty. As Alice Cherki notes in her biography, there is in Fanon a constant back-and-forth between feeling disappointed and let down by others, and still wishing to believe in them at all costs and retain a connection.[15] The result is a curious Fanon paradox: an obsession with death allied to an all-consuming rage to live. If it is the case that Fanon knew early on that he was going to die young and so had to 'live life fast',[16] such premonitory certitude also gave him the strength to leap again and again into the fire of the unknown and to act resolutely and decisively. Yet it also generated a latent anxiety, for he would always dream, in a lay version of Christian redemption and resurrection, of a heroic death that would transform his life into destiny.

Whatever potentially lethal mission Fanon was referring to in his letter never materialized, and three months later Germany capitulated. On 18 May he was demobbed and returned with Manville to Toulon for the Liberation. What should have been a moment of relief and celebration turned into yet more disappointment, however, for he was forbidden from going into Toulon on his own. And when he was there with his company he found that French women did not wish to dance with a *nègre*, even one splendidly dressed in the uniform of the liberation army, preferring instead to consort with Italian prisoners of war. The valiant, victorious Black soldiers were made an object of contempt and humiliation, opening up in a distraught Fanon a psychic wound far deeper than anything he had suffered physically. He felt broken and betrayed. It was not simply that he was again looked down on by White French people by virtue of his skin colour; this was another manifestation of the military strategy of *blanchiment* pursued by the Free French leaders in line with Allied Command. Non-White soldiers were barred from taking part officially in the celebration for Victory in Europe Day, despite the fact that two-thirds of the total number of combatants had black or brown skin. Indeed, colonial troops were removed altogether from the frontlines, stripped of their uniforms and sent to holding camps before being repatriated as quickly as possible to their respective colonies.

Fanon's unit was eventually transferred north to Rouen for embarkation, although it was forced to wait a month while the Seine estuary was cleared of mines. The men were billeted in a disused country house called the Château de Chapitre in Bois-Guillaume, outside the city. One day in early September the unit commander was invited to dinner with up to fifteen of his men by a prominent businessman and member of the Resistance, Marcel Lemonnier, who lived in a large thatched house originally belonging to the château. Along with Manville, who was planning to go into law, and Mosole, who was considering pharmacy, Fanon was among those chosen, since he met the stated requirements of presentability (Lemonnier had teenage daughters). They were wined and dined in a highly personal expression of appreciation for their courage and bravery. Such a sudden and unexpected display of kindness, which moved Fanon to record in the visitors' book the 'generous hospitality and homely quality' of the occasion, provided him with one of the few positive memories of the war.[17]

The unceremonious passage home on board the *San Mateo* –
an uncomfortable commercial freight ship with scant provisions
– took 25 torturous days. There was no patriotic ceremony
to honour the soldiers when they arrived in Fort-de-France.
Instead, they were greeted with a mixture of indifference and
indignity by the civil and military authorities. Neither now nor
later in January 1946, when he was officially discharged from
the army with the rank of corporal, did Fanon wish to talk about
his wartime exploits, and he took little pride in being awarded
the Croix de Guerre. To his family he was visibly no longer the
smiling, wide-eyed Frantz of before. Going to North Africa and
France had been a scorching psychological experience of the
inhumanity of war and the injustice of anti-Black racism. He had
witnessed a desecration of the absolute ideals inculcated in him
during childhood and he felt to the core an inconsolable grief.

Yet the end of Fanon's war was also the beginning of his
new consciousness as a man who just happened to have
been born Black in a French colony. He would now prove his
singular capacity to place his emotions and anguish to one
side and focus pragmatically on his own personal survival.
The long battle for self-definition had only just begun.

3

Return to the Native Land:
With and Against Césaire

Fanon had returned to a different Martinique from the one he had left. The liberation of the island from Robert Time constituted what he later referred to as the island's first metaphysical experience and the awakening of a distinctly Martinican political consciousness (*PRA* 32, *TAR* 23). This had come about as a result of the island's allegiance to the France of the Liberation, yet after the racism Fanon had endured on metropolitan soil he was no longer sure what being French meant: he was one of many Martinicans now realizing that they were Black rather than European. In France he had been made aware of Aimé Césaire's election in May as mayor of Fort-de-France, but he remained unclear where this would really take Martinique. In the case of his own family, it was beset, like many others in the autumn of 1945, by pressing financial worries. Having been relieved of his duties during the war for being a Freemason, his father was finally resuming his work, though still resentful that his wife had been the breadwinner. Where did that leave Frantz?

The one certainty Fanon possessed was that he needed to complete his formal education and gain the *baccalauréat*. He had not been allowed to sit his oral exam at the Lycée Schoelcher during the war following an apparent argument with the principal – a situation he considered a grave injustice but that he now promptly rectified. The French government had arranged for all young returning soldiers to take their exams after only half the usual tuition period. Hence Fanon spent just five months studying philosophy, taught by M. Joseph-Henri, one of the teachers who had been less than enthusiastic about pupils joining the BMA5 and participating

Some things will always be the same: a couple dancing the *biguine* at a nightclub in Fort-de-France, 1946.

in a war for White people. The academic outcome was virtually assured, and he would take the second part of his philosophy *baccalauréat* in March 1946. At the same time he returned to playing football with his brothers, who all now belonged to the same club, L'Assaut de Saint-Pierre. His exploits on the field as a dribbler were noted in the local newspaper, *Le Sportif*. Yet the impression the twenty-year-old Fanon now gave was of a slightly withdrawn and introspective student. He was studying Nietzsche, Jaspers, Kierkegaard and Hegel and was increasingly interested in Sartre and Césaire, author of the internationally celebrated and ground-breaking long poem *Cahier d'un retour au pays natal* (Notebook of a Return to the Native Land, 1939).

Fanon had already come into indirect contact with Césaire, a Martinican native, through Joby and Manville, who had both been taught by him at the Lycée Schoelcher after his appointment in 1940. Joby had shared his notes on the exhilarating literature classes and lectures Césaire was giving, including on *poètes maudits* such as Lautréamont. Although he was never taught by Césaire himself owing to his choice of pathway in philosophy, Fanon later heralded him as the first *lycée* teacher to say the 'scandalous' words "'that it is fine and good to be a Negro'" (*PRA* 30, *TAR* 21). For Fanon, this was a radical expression and affirmation of Black identity and consciousness, and he would recite from memory entire passages of the *Cahier*. Indeed, during this formative period the status of Césaire as a cultural trailblazer held for Fanon a magical allure: he wrote poems inspired by Césaire (never published) and even considered a career in drama. Crucially, the very fact that the two never met as teacher/mentor and pupil would also allow Fanon to take a more critical stance towards Césaire when necessary.

Césaire's political activities inevitably encouraged Fanon to consider his own political views and ideals. He had arrived back in Martinique just in time to follow Césaire's electoral campaign as a communist candidate for the first Constituent National Assembly, the body charged with drafting the constitution for the Fourth French Republic. It would be the closest Fanon ever came to being part of the organized Left, but there is no evidence that he was especially sympathetic to the communist cause espoused by Césaire. He agreed with Joby when his brother highlighted an essential flaw in Césaire's campaign, namely that it never succeeded in reaching out to the peasants in the countryside (an insight that would later guide Fanon in Algeria). However, in November 1945 Césaire was firmly elected to the National Assembly as one of three *députés* for Martinique. Certain campaign speeches by Césaire – in particular those that made European civilization responsible for colonial racism, which Fanon committed to memory[1] – galvanized him into organizing a local group of Martinican youth to reconstruct the country, although decidedly not along traditional party lines. Displaying his propensity to lead and mobilize, he arranged meetings in the *communes*, incentivized young secondary school students who felt marginalized by the system, and gave a lecture on the theme of reform in the town of Sainte-Marie, on the northeast side of the island. Fanon's foray into local politics never went further than this, however, and he ultimately passed it off as merely a phase.

In truth, Fanon and Césaire were never on the same wavelength politically. Fanon judged Césaire's positions to be compromised and defeatist owing to his integrationist convictions, which commended the assimilation of Martinique into France rather than taking a stand for national independence. Indeed, governed by his overwhelming desire for Martinicans to obtain the same social rights enjoyed by the 'Metropolitans', Césaire flatly refused to endorse the growing call for a 'Fédération des Caraïbes' that would bring all Caribbean islands together. In March 1946 he steered the French National Assembly to vote unanimously to transform the colony into an Overseas Department of France (DOM), forming part of the new Union Française (French Union) created to replace the old French colonial empire system. This

Aimé Césaire speaking at a meeting organized by the Union Française in Paris, 6 June 1947, to protest against the French response to the Malagasy Uprising in Madagascar.

new status did not bring any immediate or meaningful changes to the people of Martinique, however, and several key disparities with the majority of French departments would remain, notably regarding social security payments and unemployment benefits.

For Fanon, post-war assimilation, with its repeated demands for recognition by the Other (that is, the metropole), ensured that the Antilles remained dependent on France for regional status and thus a colonial space, rather than a locus of new social, cultural and political possibilities. It was in one sense the extension, on a national scale, of *comparaison*, or the practice of continually comparing oneself with others that, according to Fanon, afflicted Antilleans whenever they met socially. He later analysed the phenomenon in *Peau noire* (*PN* 170–75, *BS* 211–16), where he writes that the Martinican does not compare himself directly with 'the white man *qua* father, leader, God' but rather 'with his fellow against the pattern [*sous le patronage*] of the white man' (*PN* 174, *BS* 215) – that is, with respect to his difference from others like himself. Fanon explained the workings of differential comparison in brutally clear fashion:

> The Negro is comparison . . . he is constantly preoccupied with self-evaluation and with the ego-ideal. Whenever he comes into contact with someone else, the question of value, of merit, arises. The Antilleans have no inherent values of their own, they are always contingent on the presence of The Other. The question is always whether he is less intelligent than I, blacker than I, less respectable than I. Every position of one's own, every effort at security, is based on relations of dependence, with the diminution of the other. It is the wreckage of what surrounds me that provides the foundation for my virility. (*PN* 170–71, *BS* 211)

Hence, while it might seem a trivial social pursuit of bragging and mocking put-downs, the culture of *comparaison* based on feelings of inferiority created a constant pressure and anxiety for Antilleans and pointed to a fundamental crisis of identity and dependency within Antillean society. Fanon goes on to note that 'Everything that an Antillean does is done for The Other . . . it is The Other who corroborates him in his search for self-validation' (*pn* 172, *bs* 212–13). Such ceaseless demand for recognition was further heightened by the fear of misrecognition (of being mistaken for West African, for example). The result was a 'neurotic' subject (and society) in active regression: 'Unable ever to be sure whether the white man considers him consciousness in-itself-for-itself, he [the Antillean] must forever absorb himself in uncovering resistance, opposition, challenge' (*pn* 180, *bs* 222).

The remorseless yet ultimately impossible search for identification by and through the Other that characterized both *comparaison* and assimilation was, for Fanon, a ticking time bomb into pathology. The only way out of such a pernicious continuum was a definitive break, that is, revolutionary action – the argument of his future work *Les Damnés*. He thus strenuously dissented when, much later, Césaire invited Martinicans to vote 'yes' on a constitutional referendum declared by de Gaulle in September 1958, which he viewed as yet another self-defeating assimilationist trap. Forming in the same year his own Parti Progressiste Martiniquais, which favoured the autonomy of Martinique within France, Césaire would safely retain his seat in parliament until 1993.

It was, however, on the more cultural and philosophical aspects of Black consciousness that Fanon and Césaire were most fundamentally opposed. Along with the Senegalese poet Léopold Sédar Senghor and French Guianese poet Léon-Gontran Damas, Césaire was one of the founders of the Négritude literary movement of the 1930s and '40s, which Fanon immediately admired for its commitment to anti-colonialism. The term *négritude* had first been used by Senghor in 1936, then by Césaire in *Cahier*, both to convey the universal value of Black or African culture and identity, and to champion an essential sensibility and rhythm shared by all Black people across the globe. Senghor even claimed, romantically, that 'emotion is completely Negro as reason is Greek' ('I wade in the irrational. Up to the neck in the irrational. And now how my voice vibrates!' [*pn* 99, *bs* 123], as Fanon ironically glossed it). Césaire had sought to nuance the notion of *négritude* in the literary review

Tropiques that he founded in 1941 with his wife, Suzanne, and other Martinican intellectuals and which, while comprising elements of Surrealism, psychoanalysis and anthropology, sought to address Martinican realities. Fanon may not have read the journal, which had been banned in 1943 by Admiral Robert, but he knew of its existence and that it followed in the path of the earlier journal *Légitime défense*, founded in 1932 by young Black Martinican intellectuals such as René Ménil (also a teacher at the Lycée Schoelcher), which reflected on Martinican literature and identity. Césaire rightly considered *négritude* a vital stance against European fascism. When the head censor in Vichy prevented him and his fellow editors from publishing *Tropiques* on the grounds that it was racist, they countered in a letter dated 12 May 1943 that they were indeed 'racists', but 'of the racism of Toussaint L'Ouverture, Claude McKay, and Langston Hughes – against that of Drumont and Hitler.'[2]

If Fanon fully respected the ideological motivation behind Césaire's affirmatory claims for *négritude* within the context of the period, attested by his fulsome tribute to Césaire in the 1955 essay 'Antillais et Africains' ('West Indians and Africans'; PRA 26–36, TAR 17–27), the appeal of *négritude* to racial authenticity and exceptionalism always troubled him, and he ultimately regarded it as both an intellectual and political dead end. However much he admired Césaire's stunning mastery of language, he saw the 'attitude, so heroically absolute' (PN 11, BS 16) of *négritude* as a form of self-denial, since it appeared locked in a mythical past and unwilling to capture both the dynamism of present, lived experience and its capacity for transformation. In *Peau noire*, which engages with a number of texts by Césaire, including *Discours sur le colonialisme* (1950), Fanon makes a number of disparaging references to *Cahier*, which he viewed as evidence of a naive and deluded belief that the world would suddenly open up and political tensions and tribal rivalries magically fall away once local and national borders of language and culture were transcended by a universal Black culture. He also dismisses any temptation to believe in a 'natural' identity, racial or otherwise, stating sardonically: 'I am a Frenchman, I am interested in French culture, French civilization . . . I am personally interested in the future of France, in French values, in the French nation. What have I do with a black empire?' (*PN* 164, *BS* 203).

Fanon is not consistent in *Peau noire*, however. Initially he upbraids Sartre, who, in his important preface to Senghor's anthology of African writing, *Orphée noir* (1948), had described *négritude* as a mode of 'anti-racist racism' and a 'weak moment in a dialectical process' focused on a society free of race and class oppression. According to Fanon, Sartre had too easily relativized things. Approaching *négritude* positively as a *strategic* form of essentialism (it is the Negro, after all, who creates *négritude*), Fanon denounces Sartre's error: 'That born Hegelian [Sartre] had forgotten that consciousness has to lose itself in the night of the absolute, the only condition to attain to consciousness of self' (*PN* 108, *BS* 134). Yet by the end of *Peau noire*, Fanon recognizes the same basic limitations of *négritude* as Sartre, noting in particular that it presents a simplified account of the many complex and different modalities of ethnic being. As Jane Hiddleston suggests in her reading of *Peau noire*, there can be 'no single set of "black values" since black identity is inevitably mobile and changeable, and the notion of any kind of black specificity entails a determinism that reduces and glosses that variability.'[3] Yet Fanon's anti-essentializing argument and ethics also chime paradoxically with Césaire's own vision of *négritude* as a dynamic movement of reinvention and creativity – that is, of a new 'alternative ontology, that refuses to allow Being to attain the mastery and stasis of Totality'.[4] Hence, if Césaire writes of a return to the native land, this should be perceived less as a movement backwards towards origin and essence than a process of self-recreation.[5] Likewise, Fanon aims to move beyond what he called 'History' as created and defined by colonialism, whereby the Black man is condemned to an overdetermined negative sphere, by founding a new, *universal* human time and consciousness that escapes the impasse of identarian recourses to being either all Black or all White.

If Fanon was already by 1946 ambivalent about the misguided presuppositions of *négritude*, his ongoing conflicted engagement and negotiation with *négritude* ideals, including embracing its original emancipatory impetus when it suited, constitutes one of the central planks of his thinking. Moreover, although he grew increasingly frustrated and disenchanted with the political situation in Martinique and the impossibility of radical change and independence which Césaire represented (Césaire would remain mayor of Fort-de-France until 2001), Fanon continued to draw on the sheer brilliance of Césaire's extraordinarily rich and powerful poetry and theatre, tapping into its explosive energy and bounteous supply of vivid, often bloody and hallucinatory images and metaphors, notably in the historical drama *Et les chiens se taisaient* (1946; And the Dogs Were Silent), which covers the events of the Haitian Revolution and the tragic destiny of its leader, Toussaint L'Ouverture, and which contains the prophetic phrase 'kill the whites'. Fanon's particular issues with Césaire's use of pidgin and words of his own coinage are still of aesthetic and political interest, notably for the contemporary African American poet and scholar Fred Moten, who reveals the new dimensions that this debate has acquired over time. For Moten, reading Césaire's poetry today with a stronger sense of the historical specificity of his writing provides the present with the kind of historical investigation of Blackness that Fanon felt was unavailable. For Moten, the fact that Césaire achieved this through the materiality of language indicates Blackness's power for a new 'communicability' not rooted in an essentialized idea of race, but rather in new methods of critiquing the cultural machinery that essentializes.[6]

As for Césaire, he understood Fanon well despite their ideological differences and divergences, which never destroyed their mutual respect for each other and their generally affable personal relations. In a tribute to Fanon following his death, Césaire wrote: 'As a doctor, he [Fanon] knew human suffering. As a psychiatrist, he observed the impact on the human mind of traumatic events. Above all, as a "colonial" man he felt and understood what it was to be born and live in a colonial situation.'[7] In a poem about Fanon that draws on the meaning of the French word *fanon* (a noun signifying a whalebone plate or blade), Césaire hailed him as a 'flint-warrior' ('guerrier-silex')[8] – a striking formula that captures both the granite of Fanon's political idealism (the inflexibility of his commitment to decolonization) and the incandescence of his revolutionary fire. As Césaire put it well in his tribute, in which he presents Fanon as an epic and tragic figure (a 'paraclete' without its religious dimension), Fanon's revolt was ethical because he approached life as the transformation of thought into action: 'No one was more respectful of thought, nor more responsible with his own thought, nor more exacting towards life, which he couldn't imagine in terms other than of thought turned into action.'[9] Further, Fanon's violence was 'the violence of justice, of purity, of intransigence', owing to his 'absolute passion' for justice. In short, 'Just as this man of violence was an agent of love, so this revolutionary was an agent of humanism!'[10]

This was all for the future, of course. For now Fanon realized that, if he was going to make something of his life and aspire to a career on his own terms, he would, like Césaire, need to leave Martinique, where there were no real prospects. France was certainly not the promised land socially and economically, disrupted as it was by strikes and continued rationing in the immediate aftermath of war. Yet going to university in France was for Fanon and other Martinicans of his class a further stage in being French (that is, becoming White), and, despite his disenchanting experiences of the metropole that had denied his very humanity and treated him like an outsider, he still felt intrinsically French. The legislation of 4 August 1945 had given war veterans the right to free tuition and small maintenance grants awarded by the Conseil Général. He applied to the commission and was successful in obtaining a scholarship to study in France.

Now 21 and, following a delayed puberty, fully developed, Fanon was of good stature, with a long face, a strong, wide jaw and deep-set, probing eyes – the very picture of a sharp, talented young man poised for action. The sense of raw ambition was all the greater for the fact that no one in his family had yet been to university. He decided on a career in dentistry, since this would best guarantee money and status. The obvious place to study was the Paris School of Dentistry. And so, in September 1946, Fanon found himself again on a boat bound, inexorably, for the belly of the beast.

4

The Voyage In:
Love and Loathing in Lyon

Fanon arrived in Le Havre on the steamer *Colombie* with his sister
Gabrielle, who was also going to France to study pharmacy. After
helping her get settled in Rouen, where he introduced her to the
Lemonnier family who had been so hospitable to him the year
before, he headed to Paris, specifically the rue Blondel in the 2nd
arrondissement, an area of decrepit buildings and brothels where
students from the colonies like his friends Manville and Mosole
were already eking out an existence. He started introductory
courses at the School of Dentistry but lasted just a matter of
days. Fanon cited boredom as a reason for giving up, although his
decision had probably more to do with his living environment:
he did not wish to be segregated in an all-Antillean enclave
(which also numbered communists and Trotskyists) and so end
up rehearsing the standard moves of *comparaison* – that is, the
insatiable demand for self-validation and recognition dependent
on the Other. Nor did he wish to risk what he later theorized as
the 'Antillean Umwelt' (*PN* 29, *BS* 37), a defensive response to racial
discrimination that caused Antilleans to withdraw from French
society. His desire was to confront French society head-on, and
on his own terms, in order to attain a new level of consciousness
in his life not defined by race. 'The less I see of them [*les nègres*],
the better I feel,' he provocatively declared, adding ironically,
according to Manville: 'I want to whiten myself [*me lactifier*].'[1]

In one respect, of course, Fanon was simply following the model
established by Black intellectuals of Césaire's generation, whose
displacement from one colonial space to another provided the

opportunity to develop an anti-colonial consciousness. In what Edward Said later called 'the voyage in', Third World students and intellectuals moving into the metropolitan realities of the First World experienced first alienation but then radicalization – in the case of assimilated, middle-class *évolués* of the Antilles, by directly challenging the link between Blackness and Frenchness.[2] But Fanon customized the template: in typically impulsive fashion, he abruptly decamped to Lyon, where he enrolled in the Faculty of Medicine. He flirted first with the idea of becoming a surgeon, but dissection put him off (since childhood the sight of raw flesh had churned his stomach to the point of nausea). In another rapid cast of the die, he chose psychiatry, which required a preparatory year in chemistry, physics and biology.

Why Lyon? After all, apart from his *marraine de guerre* and the friends he briefly made in Nantua while recuperating during the war, he had no connections with the city, which was conservative, bourgeois and notoriously unfriendly to foreigners of whatever colour skin. Accommodation could certainly be cheaper in provincial towns, but in Lyon there was a similar housing shortage to that in Paris, and Black students were regularly denied lodging and services. Finding his place professionally in Lyon would also

A postcard view of the Place de la République in Lyon's 2nd arrondissement, 1946.

prove challenging, for the university was, comparatively speaking, a psychiatric desert: there was no chair in psychiatry, which was marginalized within the medical faculty. Finally, on a practical level, it would not be so easy to get to Rouen to visit Gabrielle. Yet Fanon genuinely hoped that Lyon would provide him with the necessary conditions for integrating into French society and culture and so advance his fundamental aim of existential autonomy.

The reality of Lyon soon disabused him of such naivety. He was obliged to live in borderline poverty in a former brothel at 29 rue Tupin in the 2nd arrondissement, recently requisitioned by the Ministry of Education for student housing. His first months at the faculty were grim: he was one of only thirty Black students in a class of four hundred. Older and with more experience of life, he found his peers callow and abusive; they in turn considered him sullen and prickly and made him the butt of racist insults and slurs such as *blanchette* (the feminine diminutive of *blanc*, 'white'). Fanon, who could be sharp-tongued and ferocious in arguments, which he sought always to win, would characteristically fight back, including, during one autopsy class, in supremely physical fashion. However, his displays of aggression served more to defend himself against his own insecurities and doubts. He was eventually left alone, leaving him yet more isolated. More generally, life in Lyon, even at its most apparently pleasant, was a series of micro-aggressions and unwanted scrutiny: from condescending compliments on his French to benevolent praise of his intellect. He later recalled how, following a lecture he gave in Lyon on the parallels between Black and European poetry, one metropolitan acquaintance remarked enthusiastically that he was 'at bottom . . . a white man' (*AF* 30, *BS* 38) – as if he couldn't be both Black and eloquent. Such was the daily reality of racial classification in France based on racially exclusive notions of national identity, whereby non-Whites were relegated to the category of non-citizen, even non-human.

Academically at least, Fanon was firing on all cylinders, taking in addition to medicine courses in literature and sociology. With the preparatory year successfully completed, he entered the university's medical school for the next four years of study and earned good marks and respect from his professors. He pursued his interests in philosophy and literature, and read existential thinkers such as Husserl, Heidegger and Sartre, as well as Marx, Hegel, Kojève, Nietzsche, Emmanuel Mounier, Kierkegaard, Jaspers, Bergson, Bachelard, Marcel Mauss, André Leroi-Gourhan, Levinas and Freud. He also attended lectures by the Catholic philosopher Jean Lacroix and the phenomenologist Maurice Merleau-Ponty, whose influential examination of embodiment and lived experience had a powerful impact on him. It was only in his fourth year that Fanon specialized in psychiatry, under the supervision of Professor Jean Dechaume, who was based at the Hôpital de Grange-Blanche. Dechaume was interested in psychosurgery, neuropsychiatry and neurology; social psychology, like psychoanalysis, was virtually unknown in Lyon.

Despite the material hardships, perennial lack of money and constantly being the casual object of racism in an almost entirely White world, Fanon was availing himself of the various opportunities offered by Lyon while also creating his own. He frequented bookstores such as Les Nouveautés on the Place Bellecour, a meeting place for young socialists and communists, attended left-wing meetings, toured occupied factories and participated in anti-colonialist demonstrations, including one demanding the release of the head of the Communist Party of La Réunion, Paul Vergès, who was jailed for several months in Lyon in 1947. (In the ensuing violence Fanon was among those beaten by police batons.) He also went to the theatre, in particular the Théâtre des Célestins, where he saw the politically engaged drama of Sartre and Camus, and the Théâtre de la Comédie, with its early stage productions by Robert Planchon. He was particularly friendly with fellow Martinican Louis-Thomas Achille, who in 1948 founded the Park Glee Club, a student choir devoted entirely to singing spirituals. Although not a musician himself, Fanon enjoyed contemporary Black music and went to jazz and blues concerts. He helped set up the anti-colonial Overseas Students' Association and wrote essays for *Tam-Tam*, a short-lived journal of overseas university students, which published its only issue on the occasion of an 'anti-colonial day' (21 February 1948). He was a devotee of the major journals, such as *Les Temps modernes*, *Esprit* (the voice of the Catholic Left) and the recently founded *Présence africaine* which, although not a political organ, would soon become a hub of the Black community in France, with its publishing house and bookstore in Paris's Latin Quarter. He was also reading in translation the novels of African American writers such as Richard Wright and Chester Himes.

Another favourite pastime was watching popular French and American films, even if the experience of going to the cinema caused him excruciating anxiety. When Black characters appeared on screen he felt he was meeting himself, owing to the colour of his skin, while at the same time interiorizing the White gaze. He later wrote of this destabilizing experience, which left his self-image shattered from the outside: 'I cannot go to a film without seeing myself. I wait for me. In the interval, just before the film starts, I wait for me. The people in the theatre are watching me, examining me, waiting for me. A Negro groom is going to appear. My heart makes my head swim. The crippled veteran of the Pacific war says to my brother, "Resign yourself to your colour the way I got used to my stump;

Peter Moss (James Edwards) provoked into walking by the army psychiatrist (Jeff Corey) in *Home of the Brave* (1949).

we're both victims'" (*PN* 113, *BS* 140). Fanon is referring here (not wholly accurately) to *Home of the Brave* (1949; dir. Mark Robson) about an African American soldier called Peter Moss experiencing racial discrimination while serving in the South Pacific during the Second World War. In the film's climax, Moss's White psychiatrist forces him to overcome his paralysis (caused by emotional shock and extended abuse during a mission) by yelling at him a racial slur so offensive that he is compelled to rise and walk. Another film that left a lasting mark on Fanon owing to its deployment of racist stereotypes of Black people was *Crash Dive* (1943; dir. Archie Mayo), featuring an African American crewman in a submarine who, in the badly dubbed French version, 'talked in the most classic dialect imaginable . . . he was all *n*[****]*r*, walking backward, shaking at the slightest sign of irritation on the part of a petty officer; ultimately he was killed in the course of the voyage' (*PN* 27, *BS* 34; original emphasis). The acute emotional discomfort Fanon experienced watching such films in a public setting would profoundly shape his future theories about Black subjectivity, identification and alienation in colonial society.

In February 1947 Fanon received a telegram announcing his father's death the previous month at the age of 56. Overwhelmed by this sudden and unexpected loss, especially after the rancour caused by his vituperative letter from the front, he rushed to Rouen to support Gabrielle. He had, after all, never broken his close affective ties with his family, who continued to provide a bedrock of security and unconditional love. Indeed, during the whole period he was in Lyon, Fanon was writing letters to his mother in which he professed upset at not hearing more from his other siblings. At times he would express, with calculated touches of heightened emotion, how spiritually low and alone he felt. His childhood had made him a social creature who was naturally happier in company, and he never functioned well on his own, making the daily constrictions on social mixing in Lyon on account of skin colour even harder to bear. In other letters to his *marraine de guerre*, in which he articulated his regret for committing the 'sin' of coming to Lyon, he displayed a distinct tendency to catastrophize:

Fanon at the Stade Géo André in Paris while visiting his brother Joby in 1949.

'I've become accustomed to detaching myself, detesting everything, hating everything.'[3] Temperamentally, Fanon could veer from being one day ardently idealistic and bullishly optimistic for a better future, to feeling utterly dejected and downcast the next.[4] The situation was magnified by his insufficient grant, although Joby, now studying law in Paris, did send him money occasionally to allow him to cover his rent and eat in the student canteen. Fanon also made frequent trips to visit Joby, first in Paris, then later in Lauterbourg and Dunkirk. All the while he was slowly drifting apart from his initial circle of friends in the rue Blondel. However, during his increasingly rare visits there, he continued to enjoy drinking rum, dancing the *biguine* with the records of his youth (in particular those by the Martinican clarinettist Alexandre Stellio, father of the Marseille *biguine*) and eating saltfish accras (his nickname was 'Dachin', from the Antillean vegetable dish *le dachine*, that is, cooked dasheen or taro).

It was to Joby that Fanon automatically turned in 1948 to discuss his liaison with a Russian Jewish medical student in Lyon called Michèle Weyer, aged eighteen but still officially a minor, which had led to the birth of a daughter. Although student circles in Lyon were racially mixed, they were rarely sexually mixed between Blacks and Whites, so this was exceptional. Since abortion was illegal, Michèle was forced to have the baby, thus putting paid to her own medical career. Yet Fanon's personal circumstances meant that marriage was out of the question for him: the occasional subsidies that Joby provided were insufficient to support a child. Moreover, dreading the 'larval, stocky, obsolete life' that awaited him in Lyon on completion of his studies, he did not aspire to 'marriage, children, a home, the family table'.[5] The relationship between the two came to an end. In July 1948, while visiting their brother who had the offer of a flat in Nantua for the vacation, Joby and Gabrielle insisted on meeting the little girl, called Mireille, who was being cared for by a wet nurse on the outskirts of Lyon. Fanon provided the address but did not join them, although he expressed his delight when he was informed that she was a lovely *métisse* girl with a jolly face, a little like their younger sister Marie-Flore (who herself would later come to Lyon to study). He would never meet Mireille and never talked about her again, except three months before his death in 1961 when he enquired after her. According to Joby, Fanon was always troubled by the silence he maintained over her existence. Yet the fact that he legally acknowledged her birth ensured that she could use his surname in later life, which she duly did.[6]

Another reason Fanon had not wished to marry was that he had already fallen for someone else: an eighteen-year-old fellow student studying literature and classics called Marie-Josèphe (Josie) Dublé, a native of Lyon but of Corsican descent, hence not a typical metropolitan White woman. She was attractive, slim and dark-haired, her large brown eyes, curved lip and contralto voice suggesting a certain mystery and sensuality. With her vivacious character and brazen humour she appeared a good match for Fanon, who could also turn on the charm when required, fully conscious of the power of his personality and his masculine good looks and stylish demeanour. They went to see plays together (Fanon would later claim that they met on the steps of a theatre), yet such was the prevailing racism in Lyon that he was often harassed while out walking with her, and at one stage even accused of being her pimp. By contrast, Josie's parents – left-wing trade unionists working in the postal services – wholly embraced Fanon. When they were at ease in his student flat, Josie encouraged Fanon's literary and artistic side. He soon began to dictate to her his writings, which he composed without notes while pacing up and down as if delivering a lecture. He declaimed rapidly and as if spontaneously, in vigorous cadences, allowing the rhythms of his body to guide his thoughts. He rarely needed to correct or revise his words. Such highly muscular and intuitive 'live' writing – the charged material process of words becoming ideas in a passionate drive towards sense and legibility – served to forge Fanon's distinctive literary style.

The Writerly Turn

One of Fanon's first essays, entitled 'The "North African Syndrome"' (published in 1952 in *Esprit*), focused on the health and conditions of the isolated and impoverished community of North African workers crowded into the small flats and slums on the rue Moncey in central Lyon. Many of the men complained of diffuse yet persistent, even deathlike, pains that could not be medically explained, leading doctors to classify them as an imaginary illness – or asymptomatic 'North African syndrome'. Such professional mistrust reflected the common prejudice in France that an Arab person was marked by brain and cultural defects, and so by nature 'a simulator, a liar, a malingerer, a sluggard, a thief' (*PRA* 15, *TAR* 7). Yet Fanon could see from his research that these men were suffering from a psychosomatic disorder caused by indisputable material, social and cultural factors: 'Threatened in his affectivity, threatened in his social activity, threatened in his membership in the community – the North African combines all the conditions that make a sick man' (*PRA* 21, *TAR* 13). Proceeding systematically via a series of 'theses' that are carefully broken down and interrogated, Fanon revealed how French medicine approached Maghrebi immigrants with 'an *a priori* attitude' (*PRA* 15, *TAR* 7) not derived 'experimentally' but rather 'on the basis of an oral tradition' (*PRA* 18, *TAR* 10). 'The North African does not come with a substratum common to his race,' he argued, 'but on a foundation built by the European. In other words, the North African, spontaneously, by the very fact of appearing on the scene, enters into a pre-existing framework' (*PRA* 15, *TAR* 7). Fanon is addressing here the harmful effects of immigration and marginalization on the psyche. He understood that the afflictions of the North Africans were real: they were both segregated in the city and exiled from their own culture, and their permanent experience of social and political negation as subhuman '*bicots*' (literally, 'kid goats') or '*ratons*' (literally, 'little rats') resulted in their silent suffering. Fanon's approach here – less a clinical description of a specifically African sickness than an account of the total dehumanization and rejection of a particular group of men by a racist medical profession that aggressively and contemptuously demanded an exact symptom – was at once radical and revelatory.

Fanon's early writings were not only scientific, however. In 1949 he wrote two plays, *L'Oeil se noie* (The Drowning Eye) and *Les Mains parallèles* (Parallel Hands); a third called *La Conspiration* (The Conspiracy) has since been lost. They were never published or performed: Fanon sent them to the renowned actor and director Jean-Louis Barrault in Paris but never received a reply. He also typically never talked about them later in life. However, at the time Fanon was immensely proud of these serious, intricate dramas, since they were the result of a period of intense reflection and introspection. They indicate in concrete and fascinating ways some of the primary intellectual ideas and influences Fanon was exploring – in particular Sartre and Césaire, but also Nietzsche, Kierkegaard and Camus – and his attempt to address prevailing existentialist preoccupations with lived experience and consciousness, identity and action, as well as the relations between the everyday and the absolute. While not set explicitly within the colonial context of race and racism, they each explore issues of disalienation and (self-) transformation, and disclose personal aspects of Fanon and his imagination, including his obsession with death and incipient feelings of revolt. They ultimately pose the key question: does one assimilate or contest?

In *L'Oeil se noie* the characters are presented in terms of their skin colour: Lucien, a sensualist, is 'the colour of pewter'; his brother, the visionary François, is the 'colour of blotting paper'; Ginette, the object of their rivalrous affection, is the 'colour of a drop of rain'. François, around whom the play revolves, sees himself as both Black and White (Black but not *nègre*; culturally White because European). Fanon is addressing here alienating stereotypes about racial identity: there are references to 'whiteness' and *la mort blanche* (literally 'white death', a medical term for cases during autopsy where the cause of death cannot be determined). In Sartrean terms, Lucien is motivated by *l'être-pour-soi* and savouring life, while François's quest is for *l'être-en-soi* and authenticity (his dream about being lynched directly echoes Sartre's 1946 play *La Putain respectueuse* (The Respectful Prostitute), which takes place in the American South). Yet *L'Oeil se noie* is also in part a critique of Sartre, whose influence is counterpointed – in phrases such as 'the abyss where the eye drowns' – with the Nietzschean model of self-affirmation and exaltation of individual will and action, along with the creative destruction of inherited values. At the end François succeeds in leading Ginette towards self-completion at the gates of the Absolute, 'where life is seized', recalling also Hegel's 'night of the absolute'.

Les Mains parallèles, a four-act tragedy about regicide and revolutionary activity written in the style of ancient Greek drama, records the tragic defeat of Epithalos, who reaches the limits of the human and feels the imminent return to a form of society against which he has sacrificed his life. By the final act there is an implicit acknowledgement that the Nietzschean idea of the Superman is not realizable, thus paving the way for a more Sartrean perspective. The title is a clear allusion to Sartre's *Les Mains sales* (Dirty Hands; 1948), but there are references also to Sartre's *Les Mouches* (The Flies; 1943), *Oedipus Rex*, *Hamlet* and Césaire's *Et les chiens se taisaient*. The play ends in uncertainty, with the heroic figure now an anti-hero whose views are heavily critiqued by the strong and resolute female characters. This has been interpreted by some as an indictment by Fanon of masculine patriarchy and a wish to kill off the White Father. As Robert J. C. Young writes, the at once formal and eroticizing dialogue of *Les Mains parallèles* is grounded in the transgressive Surrealist poetics of Césaire, including its dynamic and explosive lexicon (words such as 'convulsion', 'lightning', 'orbits', 'volcanic', 'burnt-out', 'throbbing' and 'vertiginous') and the hypnotic use of exclamations and extended metaphor, anaphora and rhythmic repetition, caesura, capitalization and jarring associations (*AF* 15–18). *L'Oeil se noie* is similarly flush with emotions, physical and carnal, incorporating violence and metaphorical images of rape – as if Fanon were working intensively through Césaire in order to determine the transformative potential of language. According to Joby, Fanon in his plays approached language as 'the prelude to action':[7] 'the word must be a movement and emergence. It must be a movement sustained by movement.'[8]

Both plays were clearly informed by Fanon's own current personal experience. Fanon's later publisher François Maspero described them as a 'sort of work of personal exorcism', as if they were written to relieve the anguish he suffered in Lyon of feeling a stranger both in the White and in the Black communities.[9] For Joby, Fanon was engaging in a dialogue with himself in *Les Mains parallèles*, where the setting of Lébos was really Martinique. One might also read, as Joby did, the intense rivalry in *L'Oeil se noie* between Lucien and François (a visionary obsessed by death whom Joby regarded as double for Fanon) as a direct reference to the relationship between Frantz and his closest brother.[10] Yet in their insistence on a Nietzschean conception of the tragic and the possibility for transforming the resentment caused by powerlessness into creative power, the plays encapsulate Fanon's cardinal belief that, as Young and Jean Khalfa deftly put it, one must risk preferring unsustainable, 'unbearable, raw light' to 'the reassuring choice of obscurity without conflict'; and, in the same spirit, that one should accept the event of (self-)liberation as it unfolds over 'the comfort of the known', which is tantamount to death (*AF* 3). Equally crucial is the implication in *L'Oeil se noie* that, in a tacit rejection of *négritude*, matters of difference should be made a matter of indifference. As for *Les Mains parallèles*, its message that the transformation of consciousness and pursuit of disalienation needed to be achieved more by human means than transcendental design signals perhaps an aesthetic realization by Fanon that drama itself is ultimately incapable of fully elaborating and resolving questions of alienation and self-transformation, and that to attain the latter he would need to pursue other forms and styles of writing.

Fanon continued to remain fully engaged with his medical studies. His chosen fields of neuropsychiatry and neurosurgery seemed an appropriate option for someone who lived so much on nervous energy, but they also reflected his overlapping humanist and scientific concerns. He took one course at Le Vinatier psychiatric hospital in Lyon but decided thereafter to stay at the Faculty of Medicine under Dechaume's supervision. As part of his clinical research he experimented with free-association tests in response to racial stimuli, which he administered to hundreds of local White people over a three- to four-year period. They were like Jungian word-association tests in which the subject's immediate response to a stimulus word is interpreted as revealing. Fanon was not exploring here the unconsciousness of an individual but rather the stereotypes of a culture, hence already breaking away from classical psychiatry.[11]

In 1951 Fanon took a temporary post as house officer at the Saint-Ylie hospital in Dole, in the Jura (a train allowed him to return to Lyon to continue his Saturday ward rounds with Dechaume). It was not an auspicious start to his clinical career: he was the only doctor for over five hundred patients and was treated like a minion by his head of department, Dr Madeleine Humbert. He held firm, however, and was exposed to some fascinating cases, such as a girl with psychotic hallucinations who heard *tam-tams* and fearsome Black men, about which he would later write in terms of destructive cultural motifs manifesting a power relation between White civilization and Black 'animality' (*PN* 165–9, *BS* 209).

In the autumn of 1951 Fanon submitted his psychiatry thesis, which he successfully defended before a board of examiners on 29 November. It was a 75-page dissertation on the mental symptoms associated with a case of Friedreich's ataxia, a recessive hereditary disease of the central nervous system, based on extensive observation of a patient at Le Vinatier.[12] Although highly technical and scholarly, this was not particularly pioneering research on the causality of mental illness (it didn't need to be, of course, since it was not a doctoral thesis). It even includes the odd error in referencing, notably of Jacques Lacan's psychoanalytical work, which Fanon had discovered during Merleau-Ponty's lectures and which was largely unknown to the examiners. But this was not, in fact, the thesis Fanon had originally planned. He had first submitted to Dechaume a dissertation entitled 'Essay on the Disalienation of Blacks' – a response to the racism he had encountered in Lyon during his studies that presented the more radical socio-genetic theory he had been working on. However, it had been immediately vetoed by both Dechaume and the Dean of Faculty, not on account of its content per se, Fanon reasoned, but owing to the polemical use certain researchers might make of it. The rejected study would subsequently be published as *Peau noire*.

Structured by a tension between the tradition in which Fanon had trained and the Freudian-Lacanian discourse he had been reading, the submitted thesis sought to draw a clear scientific distinction between the role of the psychiatrist and that of the neurologist. It compared key theoreticians, namely the psychiatrist Henri Ey (author of *La Psychiatrie devant le surréalisme*; 1948), the neurologist Kurt Goldstein (the pioneer of Gestalt therapy) and Lacan, notably his 'Propos sur la causalité psychique' ('Remarks on Psychic Causality'), a speech given in 1946 in which he critiqued Ey. As Khalfa notes, what is surprising is just how much Fanon relied on Lacan's written work in freeing madness from its purely neurological setting, as well as on Lacan's establishment of madness within the realm of language and social structures and relations.[13] In fact, Fanon dedicated one-third of the thesis to Lacan's iconoclastic challenge to institutional psychiatry, endorsing his foundational position that 'every delusional phenomenon is ultimately an expressed phenomenon, that is to say, spoken' (*AF* 268). Yet in Fanon's opinion, Lacan, whom he called a 'logician of madness' owing to Lacan's ontological belief that madness resided in reason and that human madness is the possibility of freedom ('its most faithful companion'), did not go far enough and was off the mark

(*AF*, pp. 262–3). Fanon ultimately agreed more with Ey that madness is always a pathology of freedom for humans as social beings, and that the express role of the psychiatrist was to enable patients to move out of a state of alienation (the term *aliéniste* is commonly used for psychiatrists in France).

Opposing more generally Lacan's idea that mental illness is always determined psychically, Fanon adopted Ey's integrative approach founded on a clear critique of the effects of Cartesian dualism and bringing together the physical and mental. Fanon underlined the importance of the body and movement as well as spatial and social relations in the structuring of consciousness (or else its alienation if these processes are prevented), showing that, even if one finds the neurological cause of a mental condition, the illness usually only develops in a socially determined relational space that accounts for the form it takes. His final conclusion was that neurology ignored the cultural and political causality of mental pathology while traditional psychiatry underestimated it. For this reason the thesis provided a central basis for Fanon's evolving work on neuropsychiatric treatments, in which he considered the role of culture in the development of mental conditions, rejecting from the outset any naturalization of such illnesses.

Fanon never published his thesis and rarely referred to it again, although he presented a copy to his brother Félix. In his dedication he stated tellingly his 'horror of weakness' and declared that 'The greatness of a man is to be found not in his acts but in his style.' In an apparent rebuke to Joby for viewing him as a lofty idealist with his head in the clouds, he also added an epigraph from Nietzsche (chosen no doubt because of the topic, Friedreich's ataxia): 'I speak only about things *lived*, not cerebral processes' (original emphasis).[14] Fanon was, in fact, flying high and had found in psychiatry his true vocation. He would always see it so, even if his later calling was for political activism and militancy.

5

Getting Under the Colonial Skin, Leaping Out of History

When in early 1952 Fanon submitted the manuscript originally intended for his psychiatry thesis to the Paris publisher Éditions du Seuil, one of its senior book editors, Francis Jeanson, invited him for a meeting. Jeanson was a left-wing philosopher who had just published a scathing article on French attempts to 'reform' the colonial system in Algeria. He knew immediately how original and groundbreaking Fanon's study was, since it stood out from most post-war accounts of anti-colonialism, which limited themselves largely to social-economic considerations. Instead, it laid bare in concrete and visceral detail the fantasmatics of race in a totalizing system where the 'Negro' is rigidly classified and negated by the White master as an inferior and alienated Other. The text pursued a forensic analysis of the psychological wounds of anti-Black racism to both Black and White people, while mounting a brilliant critique of the psychopathology of anti-Black racism in the French colonies that were entirely reliant on the metropole (the book is presented in the opening pages as a clinical study of Antilleans).

The meeting did not go well, however. Jeanson praised the manuscript fulsomely, but Fanon thought he was being patronized and abruptly interrupted him, exclaiming: 'Not bad for a Negro, is it?'[1] The exchange played out, almost to the letter, the permanent crisis of recognition for Black Antilleans diagnosed by Fanon in the book, including the resentment they felt at being complimented by White French people for their excellent French. As a forthright man of action who spoke his mind and brooked no small talk, Fanon could appear brusque and unapproachable, in particular with people he was meeting for the first time (increasingly so if they were French). Jeanson felt insulted and angrily dismissed Fanon from his office. (He later learned that his response had earned Fanon's lifelong respect, although encounters between the two would remain awkward and friendship was not a possibility.) Fanon subsequently accepted Jeanson's suggested new title of *Peau noire, masques blancs*, and when the book was published in early summer Jeanson contributed an extensive preface hailing Fanon's 'revolutionary attitude' as well as his generous engagement with the totality of human reality, which made the work a 'concrete hymn to freedom'.[2]

While manifestly a text of self-exploration, even self-analysis (many passages are written in the first person, and reference is made to Fanon's own childhood and experience on the battlefield),

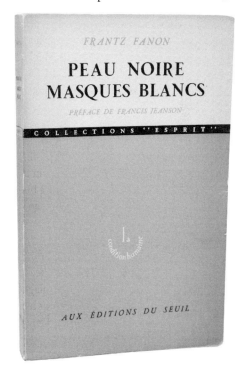

Front cover of the original 1952 edition of *Peau noire, masques blancs*.

this is not a straightforwardly autobiographical account: the often merely rhetorical 'I' incorporates a set of alienated personae and characters, in the same way that '(le) Nègre' can mean, variously, 'Blacks', 'Blackness' and 'the Black Man'. Moreover, Fanon's presentation of the colonial relation as a drama of masks clearly reflected his own writing for the stage.[3] *Peau noire* is best approached, in fact, as a form of socio-diagnostics informed by Fanon's clinical training and psychiatric research, with Fanon offering himself as his own case material. Yet it is also a highly individual and eclectic text brimming with the thousand-and-one ideas and influences swirling in Fanon's mind during his time in Lyon. Engaging with a stream of works, many only just published, he roves freely and associatively across fields and disciplines (psychiatry, phenomenology, psycho-analysis, sociology, literature, literary criticism) in order to position himself ever more finely within the major currents of intellectual thought. In addition to Sartre, the Haitian writer Jacques Roumain, Césaire and other Martinican writers, he references Chester Himes, Langston Hughes, Richard Wright and Ralph Ellison, whose *Invisible Man* was published the same year. There are also passing nods to important contemporary figures such as the ethnographer Michel Leiris, whom Fanon met briefly during this period. He cites with the express aim of supplying concrete proof in the same way that he draws on scientific evidence and data for his clinical work. Extracts from poems, novels and plays vie for attention with theories and meditations about race and colonialism, Black consciousness and subjectivity. The result is a thrilling tug and pull between science and art and aesthetics during which Fanon presents himself explicitly as a man of Reason.

The seven main chapters address thematically key areas of crisis in the Black condition: language, embodiment, gender, sexuality (including interracial relations), the dependency complex of the colonized, psychopathology and (self-)recognition. A number of theoretical dialogues are established, notably with Sartre and *négritude*, which is evoked provocatively at the start as 'the vast black abyss [*grand trou noir*]' (*PN* 11, *BS* 16). Fanon's central dialogue, however, is with psychiatry, and within that psychoanalysis, although he refers directly to Freud only twice, without indicating the provenance of quotes, and simply appropriates Lacanian terms such as the 'mirror stage' and 'family complexes'. While psychoanalysis enables Fanon to describe the transference of White fantasies onto the Black man (and, specifically, the projection of the sexual onto the abject Black body), and although Lacan's early theory of language allows him to argue that language is the colonizer's founding tool of oppression (the native may perfect the Master's language but remains alienated in the language of the colonizer at the level of vocabulary, syntax and diction for the simple fact of being Black), ultimately such theories cannot deliver a full explanation of Black alienation, the causes of which, Fanon will argue, are socially determined. He passes damning judgement on Octave Mannoni's *Prospero and Caliban: The Psychology of Colonization* (1950), an ethno-psychoanalytical work he considers dangerous since it psychologizes the colonial situation and suggests that the indigenous inhabitants were eminently amenable to colonization (that is, they had an innate inferiority complex). For Fanon, Mannoni's work exemplified the problems of applying psychoanalysis premised on the higher values of European civilization over the savage unconscious.

A key term in Fanon's introduction is 'sociogeny' (as opposed to ontogeny or phylogeny), for all elements of human being are created in the social world and thus without essential attributes. In other words, racism is a discursive rather than biological regime. The 'perverse implantation' of racist stereotypes renders self-perception alienated and dislocates the ego from the body, dividing the Black subject not only in language but in his lived, corporeal experience. He is consigned to 'a zone of nonbeing', for there is an alien other lodged inside the self, and it leads to an identification with stereo-types that may be consciously rejected but are introjected and internalized. Fanon spells out the toxic sedimentation of culture: 'I was battered down by tom-toms, cannibalism, intellectual deficiency, fetishism, racial defects, slave-ships, and above all else, above all: "Sho' good eatin'"' (*PN* 90, *BS* 112). He is referring here to the notorious 'y'a bon [. . .] BANANIA' poster for a popular chocolate drink, which depicted a grinning *tirailleur sénégalais* and the French racist idea of how an African says 'C'est bon, Banania'.

The Black man is thus caught in a catch-22: unable to represent himself to himself as White, he is also unable to represent himself as Black since he has identified himself as White from the outset. Imitating the colonizer over many years has produced a neurotic personality that, in a delirium bordering on the pathological, requires White recognition yet remains suspicious that full acceptance will ever be offered (the dilemma of *comparaison*). Moreover, the process of epidermalization provides the Black subject with what Fanon calls an alternative to the 'corporeal schema' formulated by Merleau-Ponty as a structuring of the self and the world. There is no escape from such embodiment, however many White 'masks' (for example, speaking perfect

y'a bon..

BANANIA

LE PETIT DÉJEUNER FAMILIAL

A 1950 advertising poster for Banania by Hervé Morvan.

French) the Black man may attempt to don. This is because the bodily sensations of the Black man are so 'burdened' with a 'historico-racial schema' (Fanon refers to human skin as a 'shameful livery [*livrée*] put together by centuries of incomprehension'; *PN* 10, *BS* 14) that his perception of his 'physiological self' or bodily ego is continually thrown into disarray.

If Fanon's hypotheses suggest a smooth and balanced method of investigation, the effect for the reader is of a dense, turbo-charged multi-text of rupture. The taut, elliptical opening – 'The explosion will not take place today. It is too soon . . . or too late' (*PN* 5, *BS* 9) – already destabilizes in its temporal confusion and tone of violent menace. By turns polemical, speculative, condemnatory, vitriolic, tender, sardonic, ludic, reflective, ironic and parodic, this is a boldly unpredictable, hybrid, experimental mix. The rhythms and cadences have a theatrical, declamatory ring reflecting the improvised manner in which the text was composed, with Fanon physically in motion (the downside to such 'instant', embodied writing is that ideas can sometimes appear schematic for lack of detail, and quotes and sources are not always fully noted). There are abrupt shifts in vocabulary and register between the medical and philosophical, the poetic and analytical, including use of technical terms such as 'scissiparity', 'microtome', 'excipient', 'oblativity' and 'anematize'. Fanon is effectively applying shock treatment to standard academic and scientific French, torquing it to create arresting, if at times clunky, neologisms by forming verbs from nouns, such as *inconscienciser* ('to unconsciousnessize'). He also incorporates the occasional Creole word and Martinican turn of phrase, for example *souventefois* for *souvent*, or *crabe-ma-faute* (a fiddler crab native to Guadeloupe). Injecting new energy and emotion into the language of the oppressor through syntactical, rhetorical and metaphorical manoeuvres, Fanon is imposing his poetic will on Cartesian thought and dynamiting it from within.

Fanon's unflinching wish to disarticulate the fatal, fantasized *imago* of the 'Negro' imposed by Whites on those who are summoned to introject it impels him to present, in graphic terms, the psychic injury inflicted by the White gaze. The chapter 'The Lived Experience of the Black Man' (already published as an article – Fanon's first – in *Esprit* in May 1951 as part of a special issue devoted to 'The Black Man's Complaint') begins blisteringly by citing a racist insult: '"Dirty n[****]r!" Or simply, "Look, a Negro!"' (*PN* 88, *BS* 109). It then stages cinematically a traumatic encounter extended over six pages between the narrator and a White woman and her son while travelling by train in Lyon. In what reads like a primal scene of assimilation, Fanon shows in agonizing close-up how the corporeal schema is displaced and fragmented by a racial epidermal schema that causes the body-ego to shatter. A White boy sees the narrator pass by in the aisle and fearfully announces his presence to his mother by shouting, '"Look, a Negro!"' (*PN* 90, *BS* 111), a phrase repeated three times before being expanded into, '"Mama, see the Negro! I'm frightened!"'(*PN* 90, *BS* 112). The invocation of 'Negro', already an anti-Black slur, provokes further racist insult: '"Look at the n[****]r! . . . Mama, a Negro! . . . Hell, he's getting mad . . . Take no notice, sir, he does not know that you are as civilized as we"' (*PN* 91, *BS* 113). The shock of humiliation and shame is experienced at an epidermal level as a form of dislocation generating nausea. Fanon writes of the alienating sensation of seeing himself being seen and 'overdetermined' by the boy's objectifying gaze and his and his mother's words: 'I progress by crawling. And already I am being dissected under white eyes, the only real eyes. I am *fixed*. Having adjusted their microtomes, they objectively cut away slices of my reality. I am laid bare [*trahi*]' (*PN* 93, *BS* 116; original emphasis).

Further wounds are inflicted by the woman's fetishizing attempts to classify the narrator as a 'native of "our" old colonies'. He perceives himself in triplicate, inducing a ghastly sense of self-annihilation: 'What else could it be for me but an amputation, an excision, a hemorrhage that spattered my whole body with black blood?' (*PN* 91, *BS* 112). He feels literally scorched by a Whiteness 'that burns me [*qui me calcine*]', a phrase evoking the Creole saying: 'The eyes of the *béké* burned the eyes of the negro.' On hearing '"Look how handsome that Negro is!"' he 'bursts apart' and, like a volcano suddenly exploding (Fanon's memory perhaps of the still active Mont Pelée in Martinique), shouts in incandescent rage and with calculated obscenity: "'Kiss the handsome Negro's ass [*Le beau nègre vous emmerde*], madame!'" The tables are briefly turned: 'Shame flooded her face. At last I was set free from my rumination' (ibid.).

This devastating episode of emotional and psychic violence, in which, as Stuart Hall puts it, the obligation on the Antillean to give 'a performance of self . . . scripted by the colonizer' produces in him a condition of internal splitting and total depersonalization (that is, he becomes – has no other self than – this 'self-as-Othered'),[4] presents Fanon at his most exposed and raw. There is a hallucinatory clarity and physicality to his writing here that enacts the affective rupture: the text becomes graphically jagged and fragmented, as if ripped apart by an excess of repetition, enabling the reader to feel the wounds of colonization and stigmata of racialization. At the same time the passage tropes the terms of *négritude*, for it rewrites the central moment of revelation in Césaire's *Cahier*: the 'my negritude' sequence where the Poet comes face to face with his inability to identify with the masses in the form of an enormous, poor Black man sitting opposite him on the tram. Although not explicitly referenced, Césaire's scene is clearly reframed by Fanon's first-person narrator as an instance of self-denial:

> While I was shouting that [that is, Césaire's soaring passage on *négritude* that 'thrusts into the red flesh of the soil'], in the paroxysm of my being and my fury, he [Sartre] was reminding me that my blackness was only a minor term. In all truth, in all truth I tell you, my shoulders slipped out of the framework of the world, my feet could no longer feel the touch of the ground. Without a Negro past, without a Negro future, it was impossible for me to live my Negrohood. (*PN* 112, *BS* 138)

What Fanon is prioritizing here is Sartrean existentialism, in particular his 1946 essay *Anti-Semite and Jew*, which insists that 'the Jew' as Other is an invention of the antisemite. The fundamental difference, of course, is that the Jew's being-for-others is not epidermally determined, as in the case of the Black man, and while

Sartre's antisemite fears the Jew because of his putative power, the anti-Black racist denigrates the Black person on account of his alleged deficiencies.

But if the Black body is presented as a site of diseased symptoms, it also holds the promise of decolonized revolutionary existence. Fanon's crucial insight is that, precisely because race is a discursive formation and not genetic or physiological, Blackness is neither eternal nor natural, and thus never complete: it has the potential always to be undermined and transgressed. He highlights both the historical contingency of 'Blackness' and the ways in which the oppressed can renarrate their subjectivities. Hence, despite appearances to the contrary, everything is to play for and *win* in the colonial regime, at least in theory. How, though, can a Black man be-for-himself-only when he is 'a being-for-the-Other' in a system where the internalization of the White narrative is so deep that external constraints are no longer needed? Fanon turns to the final phase of the slave's struggle for recognition in Hegel's dialectical account of the master–slave relation, which foregrounds conceptually how the master is dependent on the slave. It is the total lack of reciprocity inscribed in the positions of colonizer and colonized that opens up the necessity for confrontation and the slave's eventual struggle to the death. For Fanon, negation and death – Hegel's 'absolute lord' – make possible the restoration of the Black man's self-constituting activity, 'in-itself-for-itself'. How such a programme of violence might actually work in practice is left for the moment unresolved.

Fanon's irresistible theoretical energy is enough for him, though, to ascend at the end of *Peau noire* on the clouds of non-gendered, post-racial, universal being. In the extraordinary 'By Way of Conclusion', he reverts to the autonomous first person: 'I am not a prisoner of History. I should not seek there for the meaning of my destiny' (*PN* 186, *BS* 229). His prose becomes increasingly chiselled in a series of bullet-like mini-paragraphs that capture the axiomatic style of Descartes that he so admired. Fanon now exhibits a dazzling Sartrean sense of agency and freedom, rejecting all forms of determinism and insisting that his existential freedom is absolute and self-generating to the extent that it transcends history. The 'only solution', he declares, is to 'rise above this absurd drama that others have staged around me' (*PN* 160, *BS* 197) and reach out to the universal, the 'creation of a human world . . . of reciprocal recognitions' (*PN* 177, *BS* 218). The conclusion culminates with the triumphant statement of a universal, unified subject rendered in the minimalist form of a negative: 'The Negro is not. Anymore than the white man' (*PN* 187, *BS* 231).

Fanon's underlying project of 'authentic disalienation' (*PN* 9, *BS* 13) is now fully revealed: to liberate humankind from all determination by race and history by moving beyond identity *tout court*: 'There is no Negro mission. There is no white burden' (*PN* 185, *BS* 228). It comes down to the absolute human need for freedom and self-responsibility based on love and respect for the Other and the Other's inassimilable difference. Refusing the colonial binary of inferiority versus superiority, Fanon humbly asks: 'Why not the quite simple attempt to touch the other, to feel the other, to explain the other to myself?' (*PN* 188, *BS* 232). This simultaneous leap to the self and the Other is a new kind of perpetual self-invention beyond the colonial bounds of history, which impose merely stasis and reification, and also beyond pre-programmed narratives such as Marxism and psychoanalysis: 'I should constantly remind myself that the real *leap* consists in introducing invention into existence' (*PN* 186, *BS* 229; original emphasis). Fanon's last words celebrate both the active material body and relentless self-interrogation – 'My final prayer: O my body, make of me always a man who questions!' (*PN* 188, *BS* 232) – yet also preclude any notion that the return to the site of the body will restore an essential 'Black' subject.

Peau noire was not a success when it was published, largely because Martinique was not on anyone's political radar in France during this period of the Cold War and the war in Korea. In the few reviews the book did generate, it was considered opaque and elusive, both by the Left, which saw it as simply making a plea for equality, and by the Right, which viewed it as potentially inciting racial hatred. Communists criticized Fanon's existentialist approach to racism for being insufficiently Marxist and lacking any obvious political solution to Martinique's problems. Even the Martinican writer Léonard Sanville regarded the book unfavourably as simply reactivating positions established earlier in *Légitime défense*. But what puzzled initial readers of *Peau noire* as an uneven, motley and irrecuperable ragbag of often obscure ideas and influences cobbled together from different disciplines, shuffling and sliding between the first and third person with no clear destination, is precisely what makes it now such an original and riveting – and tantalizing – read. It is a breathtakingly 'open' and transgressive modernist text that, despite its diagnostic immediacy and propulsive energy, does not provide a clear blueprint for change: there is no sense here of the actual treatment required to heal the lethal split of Black skin and White masks threatening to destroy the Black man from within, although Fanon implies that an 'other solution' – a total 'restructuring of the world' (*PN* 66, *BS* 81–2) – may need to be violent ('For the Negro who works on a sugar plantation in Le Robert, there is only one solution: to fight'; *PN* 181, *BS* 224). Yet on a strictly personal level, how was Fanon going to build on the brief elation, forged textually in *Peau noire*, of feeling a universal subject – a subject liberated from the infernal cycle of Black social and cultural abjection – in order to create a lasting, salutary dialectic between his body and the world?

6

Socialtherapy:
The Breakthrough of Saint-Alban

In February 1952, Fanon returned to Martinique. He spent only a few months there, working as a general practitioner in Le Vauclin and earning enough money to support himself while preparing for the final postgraduate exams that awaited him in France. Although officially enrolled by the Conseil de l'Ordre des Médecins de la Martinique, he had nowhere to practise and had to rely on a makeshift surgery in the home of a family friend. It was a dispiriting experience: many inhabitants had not seen a doctor for over five years and lived in straitened circumstances. The few doctors Fanon met were corrupt and milked the system for themselves; the fact that Martinique was now officially part of France, and Césaire a communist mayor, had done little to change the system. His low spirits sank still further when the local *procureur* (prosecutor) requested that he carry out two difficult and violent autopsies, the first at the cemetery in Fort-de-France, the second at Le Prêcheur. He tinkered briefly with the idea of setting up his own psychiatric practice at the woefully under-resourced Colson psychiatric hospital to the north of Fort-de-France, yet nothing came of it. For Fanon, Martinique was increasingly a lost cause, both professionally and politically. Seeing no real sign of change, and knowing it would be hard – if not impossible – for him to be satisfied on the island, he was soon heading back to France to begin his clinical career. It was mid-March. He did not know it then, but he was leaving Martinique forever.

Back in Lyon, Fanon successfully passed his exams at the faculty of medicine and in April began a residency post at the

Saint-Alban-sur-Limagnole psychiatric hospital in the Lozère, in the remote hills of the Massif Central, to train to become a consultant. In a remarkable sealing of his future career and his growing social and political consciousness, he had the unique good fortune to find himself under the influence of the exiled Catalan psychiatrist François Tosquelles, who would guide Fanon to new horizons in experimental psychiatry and institutional psychotherapy. Fanon already knew of Tosquelles through Paul Balvet, an eminent psychiatrist at Le Vinatier and former director of Saint-Alban, whom Fanon had met via mutual friends connected to the mother of his child and who occasionally invited Fanon to dinner. Tosquelles was politically engaged: he had fought as a Republican against the Francoists in Aragon during the Spanish Civil War and had created a military psychiatric unit at the front to help combatants. Originally a religious hospital, under Tosquelles's stewardship during the Second World War Saint-Alban became a safe house for partisans and left-wing intellectuals, such as the poet Paul Éluard. However, the general condition of French psychiatric hospitals during this period was miserable, and patients had even been left to die of starvation. The internment model needed urgently to be replaced and the system modernized. Tosquelles may have been an admirer of Lacan's psychoanalytic ruminations, but he had defended his medical thesis on 'Lived Experience in Psychopathology' and now sought to transform Saint-Alban into a therapeutic community focused on survival. It developed into a pioneering laboratory for 'socialtherapy' (socialthérapie) and the heart of a psychiatric revolution that helped patients to confront reality and free themselves from their phantasms. This entailed turning the hospital into a miniature version of the outside world.

The innovation of socialtherapy (subsequently known as 'institutional therapy') rested on the core principle that not just the patients but the institution of the asylum itself needed to be cured. The way to humanize it was to promote the human value of its inmates. The disalienation of an individual's personality required taking into account their social and cultural universe of reference – that is, the world they knew outside the hospital

Aerial view of Saint-Alban-sur-Limagnole hospital, Lozère, in 1950.

setting. Tosquelles aimed to recreate within the hospital and under medical supervision the structures of external society, paying great attention to the rhythms and textures of daily life. If, according to socialtherapy, patients were alienated both medically and socially (in the case of psychosis, the cause of their alienation was biopathological and the social contract had been broken), then their care and personal restructuring depended on the creation of a structure that obliged them to assume an active role through work and group activities and, in the process, learn to reconnect with reality.

In both its material and social dimensions Saint-Alban was run jointly by the patients and the nurses, who needed thorough retraining. Moreover, working together meant coexisting in order to break down the traditional hierarchical barriers between doctors and nurses, patients and staff. In this immersive new clinical setting, based on the idea that all patients belonged as a right (in direct contrast to the authoritarian principles of imprisonment in an asylum), Tosquelles undertook to abolish the structural constraints linked to internment – not just the instruments of restraint, but forced idleness and routine. The 'club', which incorporated a film society and provided newspapers, a library and musical evenings, existed to 'transfuse' social life into the patients, who were also invited to verbalize their symptoms freely and explain their problems. A variety of therapeutic techniques were deployed – from drug therapy to electroconvulsive therapy (ECT) and psychoanalytically influenced psychotherapy – but the emphasis remained always on group work. The newly created society reintegrated patients into a form of symbolic exchange. Slowly, in managed fashion, most recovered, at least to the extent of being able to interact with one another.

François Tosquelles on the roof of Saint-Alban-sur-Limagnole hospital, holding aloft the work of a patient, Auguste Forestier, 1947.

Fanon spent fifteen months as Tosquelles's resident doctor, observing for the first time how patients could play a central part in the institution that constituted them as psychic and social subjects, and so work actively towards their own recovery.[1] Tosquelles represented for Fanon a totally new kind of model who not only straddled the separate disciplines of clinical medicine and clinical psychiatry but brought together, in new, far-ranging ways, the worlds of medicine and politics. The admiration was mutual: Tosquelles was impressed by Fanon's meticulous attention to others, his corporeal presence (the way he occupied space physically with his body and voice), and his general toughness and gift for polemic, even if that sometimes involved a certain abrasiveness (it took one to know one). Fanon had been aware of the essential role culture played in mental illness, but now he properly grasped how the act of curing renewed the link with fellow humans through an exchange of speech, enabling the patient to be reborn into the world. 'Language is what breaks the silence and the silences' (*AF* 281), he asseverated in one of his editorials for the ward journal *Trait d'union*, in which he freely combined clinical, operational and philosophical matters in strikingly personal and accessible fashion. In another editorial entitled 'Lassitude' (Weariness) stretched across two issues (nos 127–8, December 1952), which enterprisingly references the poet Paul Valéry and Luis Buñuel's 1950 film *Los Olvidados* (The Forgotten Ones), Fanon plays with self-projection for the purpose of illustration: his first-person point of view as doctor gives way briefly to that of a middle-aged man cut off from others and immobilized by anguish on account of waiting passively for life to come to him. Fanon writes vividly: 'Being weary at forty, is like saying damn to the world, to others, to life, to oneself, damn, damn, damn, to everyone.' If the psychiatrist's function was to help patients regain their normative forms of consciousness, in which the self is autonomous and in full control, then the ultimate goal of psychiatry was to produce free men. It all came down now for Fanon to a simple working formula: to treat = to cure = to liberate.

Together Fanon and Tosquelles presented three research papers at the Congrès des Médecins Aliénistes et Neurologistes de France et

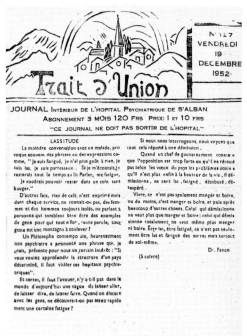

Front page of the Saint-Alban-sur-Limagnole hospital journal *Trait d'union*, no. 127 (19 December 1952).

des Pays de Langue Française in Pau in 1953. Two deal specifically with the Bini method of convulsive therapy, while the third comprises a summary of their general methods, including occupational therapy.[2] The various debates on the risks and ethics of violent intervention as a component first stage in institutional psychotherapy (that is, using ECT to reset the patient's brain for therapeutic reconstruction) are discussed in compelling detail. Maurice Despinoy, under whom Fanon also trained at Saint-Alban, noted that Fanon displayed a close interest in his own experiments with lithium salts and that, had he remained there, he would probably have written a thesis on biochemistry. Yet Fanon was at a transitional moment in his career, for although he was a qualified doctor of medicine with now cutting-edge experience in clinical psychiatry, he still had to pass the Médicat des Hôpitaux Psychiatriques, a competitive national exam (*concours*). This prestigious qualification would allow him to practise as a senior consultant. A sedulous mentor, Tosquelles helped him prepare for this obligatory next stage. (A further mark of Tosquelles's generous nature is that he even helped Fanon finance a pension for his 'lost' daughter, Mireille.)

The other part of Fanon's life during this period was, of course, Josie, who, as well as completing her own studies in Lyon and achieving a *licence* in Latin philology, was devoting herself to making a home for them. She diligently learned to cook Caribbean dishes such as *morue marinée* (pickled cod) so that he might keep his memory of Martinique alive, especially when friends such as Manville arrived – the occasion for Fanon to play his revered Stellio records.[3] The couple eventually married in Lyon on 30 October 1952, and Josie would be Fanon's life partner and closest confidant. Some questioned why he would wish to marry a White woman since in *Peau noire* he had been so damning of the Black male bourgeoisie for 'marrying white' and the phenomenon of '*lactification*' (the word in its sociological sense is Fanon's own coinage) through marriage to a White woman. He had used the example of the Martinican writer Mayotte Capécia and her *doudouiste* (folkloric) novels such as *Je suis Martiniquaise* (1948; I Am a Martinican Woman), which drew on her personal experience of being a woman of mixed race who did not see herself as Black and identified instead with Whites. Fanon dismissed her work as third-rate and symptomatic of a general Martinican fantasy of salvation through magical whitening – part of his general argument that interracial desire was pathological for Black people since it invariably took the form of a desire to be White, or at least to be in proximity to Whiteness. 'I marry white culture, white beauty, white whiteness,' he wrote in *Peau noire*, gleefully adopting the voice of a Black man craving 'total realization' through the love of a White woman – a compulsion Fanon equates with the protagonist Jean Veneuse in the autobiographical novel *Un Homme pareil aux autres* (1947; A Man Like Other Men) by the Martinican-born Black French writer Réne Maran. He added racily: 'When my restless hands caress those white breasts, they grasp white civilization and dignity and make them mine' (*PN* 51, *BS* 63).

By 'accidentalizing' her Blackness, Capécia was, according to Fanon, living in bad faith and lapsing into inauthenticity.[4] As with the ambition to speak perfect French, such desire for status in the White world was made impossible by the epidermal racial structures of colonialism and doomed the Black subject to alienation. When later in *Peau noire* Fanon adds that he wished to undertake something Capécia could not achieve, that is, 'lose myself completely in negritude' (*PN* 109, *BS* 135), he is speaking for purely strategic reasons as the 'essential' Black man. Later in *Peau noire*, however, in a highly disparaging passage on the French Jewish physician and writer Michel Salomon, whom he summarily condemned as 'racist', Fanon also declared: 'I do not feel that I should be abandoning my personality by marrying a European, whoever she might be' (*PN* 164, *BS* 202).

With the usual caveat that the first-person subject in *Peau noire* is not to be taken at face value as Fanon himself, did this apparent contradiction in his attitude to Whiteness indicate an unresolved ambivalence regarding his own Blackness, or at the very least a tension between his life and his work? After all, as he reportedly told Josie when they got married, emphasizing a central tenet of *Peau noire*, 'one is only black in the whites' gaze'.[5] Fanon never preached segregation between Whites and Blacks: his writings about the Manichean nature of the colonial world were descriptive, not prescriptive, and, as his profound concerns about *négritude* underline, he understood the dangers of Blacks being fixed in their Blackness just as much as Whites in Whiteness. He would continue in his writing to argue for a post-racial society: one where colour or nationality would be entirely immaterial to the choice of marital partner. As for Josie, who rarely spoke of her marriage to Fanon following his death, when asked in 1978 whether there was a fundamental conflict between Fanon's works, what he stood for, and the fact that he married a White French woman, she responded unequivocally:

It is my opinion, and I believe that it was also his – otherwise he would not have contracted nor remained in this interracial marriage – that there was no contradiction. In his works, he states clearly that it is through a revolutionary process that we can understand and resolve racial problems. Otherwise, we find ourselves in dead-end situations that are impossible to resolve – the sort that we can never put to rest . . . We are not going to limit each other to race! Otherwise, where is the revolution?[6]

Yet Josie's admirable wish to dispel any notion of conflict between herself and Fanon may not tell the full story of their marriage. Recent fieldwork by Félix F. Germain based on oral testimony by the late Beninese poet Paulin Joachim, who knew Fanon well in Lyon, suggests that he was regularly given to fits of violent temper and that his private life, especially his relationship with Josie, was punctuated by acts of physical violence. Joachim claims he witnessed Fanon lash out and slap her in the face, both in public and at home in front of other men, in an attempt to humiliate her, declaring in one case: 'I'm avenging myself' (no context is provided).[7] Does this claim, which has not been further substantiated, help account for Josie's guarded silence after Fanon's death? More crucially, how does it equate with the accepted notion that Fanon had an innate moral repugnance towards violence, practising it only under highly controlled medical conditions, as with ECT, and also with the abundant evidence that he respected and empowered women – not only Josie but those he came into contact with through his work and whom he encouraged to be independent and realize their full potential (women such as Alice Cherki, Elaine Mokhtefi and Marie-Jeanne Manuellan, who would figure later in his life)?

Certainly, if violence or lack of self-control was such a conflicted personal issue for Fanon and took such a toxic form, it raises serious questions about how one now reads his theories of the absolute political need for 'pure violence' and its ethical 'cleansing' properties. It also puts into heightened perspective the moments of naked masculinism in Fanon's work, as when he frankly admits of the woman of colour: 'I know nothing about her' (*PN* 145, *BS* 180) – a declaration triggered by the initial question he raises of the Black man's desire, articulated with a Freudian ring as 'What does the black man want?' (*PN* 6, *BS* 10). As Julietta Singh argues, Fanon's masculinism is born of notions of mastery: decolonization was for Fanon an act of undoing colonial mastery by producing new masterful subjects who will eventually embody the new nation-state. However, such reliance on mastery to ensure anti-colonial self-recovery produces a series of what she calls 'sacrificial figures': women, animals, disabled people, outcasts and nature.[8] One example from *Peau noire* will suffice: 'I feel in myself a soul as immense as the world, truly a soul as deep as the deepest rivers, my chest has the power to expand without limit. I am a master and I am advised to adopt the humility of the cripple' (*PN* 114, *BS* 140).

In June 1953, at the Sainte-Anne hospital in Paris, Fanon sat the exam for the Médicat des Hôpitaux Psychiatriques. He comfortably passed, impressing the examiners with his confident and precise clinical diagnosis. However, because he was ranked only 13 out of 54 applicants, he was not guaranteed a top posting and would have to wait for what became available. His first post, or 'first arms', was as a locum (*médecin-chef par intérim*) at a hospital in the small Normandy town of Pontorson. From the day in September when he arrived unannounced and was greeted by shock from the bursar, who had never before seen a Black man, he encountered suspicion and resistance. He was considered a provocateur for wishing to let his patients speak as at Saint-Alban, and he was dismissed as a sadist when he tried to practise narcotherapy (a technique learned under Tosquelles) in a darkened room. When on one occasion he authorized over thirty patients and their nurses to attend the local market, the director refused to countersign the chit. The six hundred *malades travailleurs* (working patients) employed in the hospital services under the orders of a Mother Superior (Pontorson was originally a private religious establishment) immediately went on strike. After a few tense hours, Fanon finally managed to persuade them to go back to work.

There were other systemic problems in this bleak carceral setting. When his uncle Édouard came to visit him, Fanon complained about the hopelessness of treating patients with alcoholism in this particular region of Calvados, where unscrupulous home distillers were effectively poisoning people through an illicit trade in tax-free alcohol. Yet Fanon the consummate and resourceful professional persevered, doggedly attempting to introduce new humanizing techniques while still remaining within the acknowledged parameters of psychiatry. He continued to administer ECT as a therapy if he thought it could be effective: as always, his decisions were based on operational criteria. He knew, though, that he could not stay at Pontorson, despite the fact that he enjoyed the support of a section of the staff and did not feel that the daily obstructions he encountered were directly on account of his skin colour – they had more to do with the general disarray and lack of respect within the institution. He eventually resigned and departed in late November.

Such a disheartening and abortive episode might have appeared a disaster for a newly qualified doctor starting out, yet Fanon, now 28, had already engineered his next move – one that would prove decisive. During his time at Pontorson he had applied for a post in Guadeloupe that would not become vacant before December. With little interest in remaining in the metropole, he had also considered applying for a post in Dakar, thinking that Senegal might open up a new path of psychiatric work and research between tradition and modernity. According to Joby, Fanon planned to work for a few years in sub-Saharan Africa and then transfer to his homeland – a view corroborated by a letter Fanon wrote in August 1953 to Senghor (later to become president of Senegal) expressing his desire to be sent to an African hospital, by which he meant one in Black Africa (he never received a reply).[9] Then, out of the blue, a consultant position was created at the Blida-Joinville hospital in Algeria, for which he applied. In an undated missive to Joby, Fanon wrote simply: 'I'm going to Algeria – a country where they need me,' suggesting again a certain impetuousness. Why Algeria, a country occupied by the French since 1830 but about which he knew nothing other than his fleeting wartime impression of extreme poverty? Did this resolution betray a political affinity for another country and people colonized by the same European power? Either way, his nomination was approved. On 22 October 1953 the *Journal officiel de la République française* formally announced that Monsieur le Docteur Fanon was required to make himself available to the Governor-General and Resident Minister of Algeria in Algiers, Robert Lacoste, and to take up post on 23 November.

7

Blida:
Where Medicine Meets War

Blida, the capital of Blida province, located about 45 kilometres
(28 mi.) southwest of Algiers, was a typically segregated French
colonial town: a well-laid-out modern European centre surrounded
by a loose jumble of largely neglected Arab quarters. Blida-Joinville,
Algeria's only public psychiatric hospital, was built in 1933 as a
showpiece of French psychiatry. With tree-lined avenues linking
the imposing two-storey buildings situated in a large park, it was
a virtual town-within-a-town and the epitome of colonial polish.
When Fanon arrived there in late November 1953 to begin service as
a *médecin-chef de service* (head of department), he had the immediate
impression that the well-equipped buildings were better looked
after than the patients, who were effectively regarded as incurable.
Two thousand boarders were packed into a hospital with a capacity
of just eight hundred, cared for by four *médecins-chefs* and now
Fanon, who was made responsible for 187 patients (165 European
women in one pavilion, 22 Muslim men in another). The boarders
were separated into groups (men, women, indigenous, European)
and appeared left to themselves without adequate hygiene. Fanon
even glimpsed some of them tied to their beds, others to trees in
the park.

There were multiple ironies to Fanon's position at Blida-Joinville:
he was a Black French citizen and atheist from an old colony serving
as administrator in a white gown among the Arab Muslim population
of a new colony. Speaking no Arabic or Berber, he had to rely on
interpreters. He also knew very little about recent Algerian history
and politics: the bloody events of May 1945 – when the French army,

Blida-Joinville psychiatric hospital, 1933.

aided by settlers, massacred between 25,000 and 40,000 Muslims in Sétif, Guelma and Kherrata, where nationalist rioting had broken out on VE Day – were still largely unknown in France. Yet in his first managerial role Fanon possessed the power to do what he liked (he answered only to the Governor-General) and, at least initially, he was left alone. He now had the opportunity to apply, in a different institutional setting, the experimental psychotherapy techniques he had acquired at Saint-Alban. If the field of psychiatry had been slowly changing in France, by contrast there had been almost no progress in Algeria, and few appeared interested in rocking the boat. It may not have been his original plan, but he would need to shake things up dramatically in order to reform the system, which, like the staff, appeared utterly exhausted. He had no idea what was in store for him.

In purely personal and material terms, all was looking good for Fanon: he enjoyed a good starting salary and lived comfortably with Josie in a functional villa in the grounds complete with their own car. He arrived early for work before anyone else, immaculately dressed in expensive cufflinked shirts tailor-made in Europe, carefully knotted ties, monogrammed handkerchiefs and made-to-measure white coats. He cut a dash, even changing his clothes two or three times a day to minimize the effects of heat and sweating. Although only three or four years older than most of his fellow consultants, Fanon stood out as wiser and more mature (physically, he was now sporting a gently receding hairline). They knew very little about him, other than that he had worked with Tosquelles at Saint-Alban, for his natural inclination was not to speak about his past. He also sought to keep his private and professional life separate, although he would sometimes invite colleagues to dinner, cooked by the ever-attentive Josie and accompanied by fine wines and music – the occasion for long, heated conversations (Fanon's way of decompressing).

As for the nurses, they found Fanon intimidating and distant. With his restless, often impatient demeanour and glaring, beady eyes (an effect of his myopia, which he sought to keep secret to avoid betraying personal weakness), he was an exacting taskmaster who appeared to lour over them. His combination of laconic wit and painstaking intensity could sometimes come across as bad humour and surliness. Yet Fanon was a born team leader who led by example and inspired respect and trust (even if not love) in those from whom he always expected the best. He was also highly adept at coaxing his assistants with his seductive charm and good manners. His disarming capacity for laughter – he could suddenly break out into voluble, infectious cackles – helped to keep nurses and consultants alike on side.

Fanon's first battles were inevitably with the doctrinal basis of the Algiers school of colonial ethnopsychiatry, founded by the hospital's former director Professor Antoine Porot, and its reductive racial stereotyping. This approach had been established in Algerian psychiatry circles at Mustapha University Hospital in Algiers, where, after the First World War, Porot elaborated pseudoscientific theories about the inequality of races – a mix of medical, anthropological and political half-truths based on racial prejudice – to justify the inherent racism of France's colonial mission. Porot had just one aim: to glorify the White doctor by making the Arab and Berber a subhuman characterized by a 'primitive' mentality (that is, blocked at an earlier phylogenetic stage). The notion of primitivism was promulgated by other psychiatrists including Jean Sutter, Porot's junior, who regarded Arabs as intellectually weak, violent and 'socially generous' (read: thieving, lazy, greedy, fanatical). The Berbers were one up on the Arabs, but both fell far below the White settler superman. Such White supremacist views were openly espoused by a number of Fanon's team.

In a caustic article on ethnopsychiatry published anonymously in the new anti-colonialist journal *Consciences maghrébines* in 1955, Fanon demonstrated the patently racist bases of Porot's theory with a damning use of quotes from Porot himself.[1] In addition, speaking with a new colleague, Raymond Lacaton, at the Congrès des Médecins Aliénistes et Neurologistes de France et des Pays de Langue Française in Nice in September 1955, Fanon addressed the subject of mental illness in North Africa by examining the notion of avowal in the medico-legal context. He highlighted the fact that in North Africa, while most European criminals confessed once incriminating evidence had been presented to them, North Africans rarely did, even when faced with irrefutable proof of their guilt. Nor did they attempt to vindicate themselves. The reaction of the French police and public opinion was to naturalize this behaviour by claiming that the North African was a liar by constitution. Offering a philosophical reflection on the cultural conditions and legal history of confession with reference to Sartre, Henri Bergson, Jean Nabert, Dostoyevsky and Hobbes, Fanon argued that, in this further instance of the 'North African syndrome', the silence of accused Muslims had nothing to do with cultural specificity but signalled rather their resistance to being defined as criminal by the colonial adminstration.[2]

Yet how to disalienate an entire medical institution contaminated by racist theories? Fanon was assisted by some excellent colleagues, many Jewish, including Meyer Timsit, François Sanchez, Georges Counillon (a communist *maquisard* whom Fanon had known in Lyon), Jacques Azoulay and Charles Geronimi, an Algerian-born *pied-noir* whom he personally appointed as a house officer and who became a close collaborator. He decided to put his training in social therapy into practice, starting with the wing for European women.

Within a month a community ethos was established and all the boarders became involved in organizing events and get-togethers. The first major social event was a celebration of Christmas in 1953, when Fanon let patients arrange events at which he was merely a guest and spectator. A small, one-page weekly newsletter, called *Notre Journal*, was initiated to record their collective activities, with Fanon writing the editorials. In the first number he promoted the 'most beautiful discovery' of writing as a vehicle of memory, mental organization and communication; in another he proposed the 'modern hero' as 'someone who carries out his task each day with conscience and love'. Six months later the newsletter featured its first contribution from a Muslim patient, who questioned some of the 'fictional' reconstitutive elements of socialtherapy applied at the expense of an opening up to normal social life.

Fanon knew he couldn't simply reproduce the methods of Saint-Alban, since for Blida-Joinville's indigenous patients the doctors were always *gaouris*, or Westerners. What was successful in Saint-Alban and continued to be effective for the European women under Fanon's care failed completely with his Muslim

Fanon (far right) at Blida-Joinville hospital with colleagues (including Georges Counillon at the back), end of 1954.

patients. In the indigenous male wing, the workshops didn't work at all: the men balked at basket-weaving and pottery, activities reserved for women in their culture. In the clinical papers Fanon published during this period, he candidly acknowledged the errors of his reforming plans and conceded that he had ended up simply endorsing the ideology of assimilation (in operation in Algeria since 1834, when France formally annexed the region) by expecting his Muslim patients to adapt to European culture.[3] To achieve the right operational mode there had to be 'a real and concrete investigation into the organic bases of the indigenous society' (AF 362). This required a greater awareness of Algerian society and culture and a move away from a position based on the 'supremacy of Western culture' to what Fanon termed 'cultural relativism' (AF 363). In the context of racist assimilationism, the challenge for Fanon of disalienating psychiatry quickly become one of decolonizing it. He knew that colonial society was in itself pathological and perverse, for the goal of colonization was to 'decerebralize' the native population. He thus proposed a sociological and phenomenological understanding of 'the Algerian personality' that involved replicating communal forms familiar to his Muslim patients. He set up a Moorish cafe where men felt at home drinking coffee and playing cards, then a salon in Oriental style for women. Since translators were usually regarded suspiciously by inmates as settlers or else their henchmen, Muslim staff were installed who had direct knowledge of the cultural practices of the patients and could invite local storytellers. Traditional festivals began to be celebrated, and local muftis were invited to lead Friday prayers. Fanon also worked for three months with a musician to develop a new kind of musical therapy. His enemies at the hospital covertly called him 'the Arab Doctor', but by this stage such slurs were like water off a duck's back and only hardened his resolve.

Blida-Joinville was fast becoming a dynamic centre for research, and Azoulay and Sanchez began a doctoral thesis in medicine under Fanon's supervision on the topics of djinns and dreams. Fanon himself made at least two trips into Kabylia, the Berber heartland, to study traditional attitudes towards insanity that the

French had dismissed as mere superstition. Pilgrimages were also made to *marabouts* (Muslim religious leaders or teachers) in the sacred wood of Blida, where magic amulets could be purchased for breaking a spell – part of a local system of belief in which the madman was respected and, following recovery, returned into society. In addition, Fanon consulted a *taleb* (a student in a Koranic school) and attended night-time ceremonies devoted to healing hysterics through cathartic release. Another area of interest was the cultural dimension of sexual troubles in the Muslim male population, where impotency found solutions again through the *marabout*. A number of unpublished co-written articles resulted from this research, which offered a positive though somewhat rose-coloured perspective on native Algerian society and its notions of madness as more a matter of possession by external bad spirits than of the mental personality of the 'mad' themselves.[4]

Yet Fanon remained dedicated to working on all clinical fronts, including shock treatments (ECT as well as insulin shocks for psychotic patients) and, from 1955, the use of new neuroleptic drugs and psychotropes. Treatments that had proved effective at Saint-Alban – projective thematic apperception tests (TATs), for example, which involved the description of ambiguous visual scenes on paper – fared less well with indigenous women. Their answers to the images appeared inconsistent and incoherent owing to stubborn European cultural assumptions about the psyche embedded in such tests. Throughout this period Fanon was also involved in pharmacological research, including the use of lithium citrate to treat acute mania. He even briefly experimented himself with psychoanalysis but abandoned it owing to his lack of experience with transference. However, as a psychiatrist Fanon was always acutely aware of how his mind and emotions functioned, to the extent that he could even contrive a display of anger to achieve what he wanted from obstructive administrators.

While Fanon was slowly but surely achieving major progress at Blida-Joinville and reforming the asylum from within, events were taking place outside that would quickly impinge on its development. The year 1954 was critical in the history of Algeria, since it marked the start of the war for independence. The first explosions took place in Algiers on 31 October and 1 November, although there was no sense yet that this presaged a conflict of national liberation. A month later, a small organization called the Front de Libération Nationale (FLN) carried out its first attacks and launched an armed struggle. The FLN had grown out of a split in the banned Mouvement pour le Triomphe des Libertés Démocratiques (MTLD), a centralist group championing workers' rights led by the founding father of modern Algerian nationalism, Messali Hadj. It called for the 'restoration of the Algerian state, sovereign, democratic and social, within a framework provided by Islamic principles', declaring that it would not lay down arms until this was achieved. The limited reforms introduced in 1947 under the Statute of Algeria had granted Algerian men full French citizenship and established unrestricted passage between Algeria and France. However, Arab-Berber Algerians were officially called French-Algerian Muslims (*Français-musulmans d'Algérie*), introducing an ethnically motivated subcategory of citizens, which Algerians resented. The prospects for reconciliation between Muslims and Europeans appeared remote.

In April 1955 a state of emergency was declared in Algeria and the army was granted extensive powers. The country was now under martial law. A few months later the FLN launched a major insurrection in the area around Philippeville, resulting in a dreadful massacre and reprisals on both sides. The adjoining, newly independent country of Tunisia allowed the FLN's military wing, the Armée de Libération Nationale (ALN), to establish bases on its territory. Between November 1954 and the end of 1956 there were eleven attacks on French patrols; insurgency was low-level and included sabotage raids. In response, the French established the Sections Administratives Spécialisées (SAS). The so-called 'pacification' tactics they employed involved trying to divide the 'sane' population from the rebels and to exploit the rivalry between the FLN and another Muslim group, the Mouvement National Algérien (MNA). From 1956 onwards the arrival of an accelerating number of fresh French conscripts allowed for the establishment of more checkpoints and static units. So began a period of blanket repression, including indiscriminate sweeps, the deportation of over two million Arabs (almost a quarter of the entire population) to internment camps, the staging of massacres subsequently attributed to the FLN, and wholesale torture and killing by the Renseignements Généraux (RG).

Nothing dictated that Fanon would feel committed to joining a long-haul military struggle for independence. After all, he had so far resisted aligning himself with a political party, and Blida-Joinville was potentially only a stepping-stone in a distinguished medical career that might take him anywhere in the Francophone world where he could develop his innovatory practice in psychiatry. Yet it was already clear from *Peau noire* that Fanon was convinced of the need for a complete – and, if necessary, violent – overhaul of all social structures under colonialism. His fervent critique of medicine as a tool of colonial violence had led him to foreground the psychic impact of colonialism, and he could see that, for the colonized in Algeria, the most serious problem blocking the path to self-realization and freedom was psychic and social alienation. Moreover, on a purely personal level, participation in a revolutionary collective project might offer him the chance for self-renewal and transformation, potentially even the heroic encounter with destiny denied him on the battlefield during the Second World War. His instinctive thought was to fight on the frontline and join the *maquis*, or resistance movement. This never happened, although he did make a point of speeding towards police roadblocks in his Simca in a wilful and unusually reckless public display of insolence.

Hence the Algerian war of liberation represented also a watershed moment for Fanon, and when the nationalist rebels made initial contact with him in early 1955 to enlist his support, he needed little convincing. His first encounter was through members of the small humanitarian association Amitiés Algériennes, which had grown out of the Association de la Jeunesse Algérienne pour l'Action Sociale (AJAAS), the publisher of *Consciences maghrébines*. Its editors, including the Catholic historian André Mandouze, who taught classics courses at Algiers University (attended by Josie), provided assistance to the FLN *maquisards* of the Algérois in the north, specifically *wilaya* (region) IV. After contributing material to *Consciences maghrébines*, Fanon was put in touch with nationalist militants including Pierre Chaulet, a young left-wing French Catholic doctor who invited him to give talks on the theme of 'Fear and Anxiety' for AJAAS members.[5] It was through the AJAAS that Fanon also met Alice Cherki, a promising young medical student in Algiers interested in psychiatry, who eagerly accepted his proposal that she train at Blida-Joinville. One day Chaulet asked if he would be willing to receive ALN soldiers suffering mental pathologies at the hospital; Fanon immediately agreed on behalf of himself and his new co-director, Lacaton. This led in turn to his encounter with the local FLN commanders Si Sadek (*nom de guerre* of Slimane Dehilès) and Azzedine (*nom de guerre* of Rabah Zerari), who had heard of his experimental and politicizing methods with the Arab 'mad' and his creation of an 'open-service' day clinic to allow for temporary boarders (that is, patients suffering light pathologies such as depressions). Knowing a psychiatric hospital would keep the police and army outside its gates, they suggested he could hide *maquisards* and young FLN sympathizers gathered in the Chréa mountain near Blida and make up prescriptions for the FLN field hospital with the help of his pharmacist. Fanon promptly obliged. The war for independence was now also his war.

Blida Ground Zero

Fanon's daily routine changed dramatically overnight. A force of nature with prodigious energy, he was now in overdrive. He had regular contacts with the military of the ALN, 'treated' respectable-looking Arabs who were serving as messengers between the hospital and the FLN of *wilaya* IV, allowed clandestine FLN meetings to be held at the hospital, transmitted information, hid weapons and forbade the police from entering with their guns loaded. He was also soon teaching fighters how to manage their body language when placing a bomb and how to resist torture. Research trips to Kabylia became undercover work in the field. Above all, Fanon was dealing with a continuous flow of traumatized men, some with psychosomatic complaints, others suffering from either reactive or situational psychoses. By day he treated the French torturers, by night the Algerian tortured: he treated all equally and in strict confidence. During his regular rounds important information was occasionally revealed by patients, in one case by a French woman about a potential attack her soldier husband (André Achiary) was planning on the prime minister, Guy Mollet, by using criminal elements from the traditional Arab quarter of the Casbah in Algiers to make it appear an FLN attack. Fanon was obliged to pass the details on to Mandouze, who had links to the government, in order to avoid the murder of innocents, but he let his patient know exactly what he had done.

Fanon could clearly see that the psychiatric disorders suffered by Algerians were the result not just of political violence, racism, torture and murder, but of the permanent situation of social and economic deprivation, oppression and internment. It seemed, therefore, increasingly futile to treat patients only to send them back into the same environment. What had to be changed was not the people but the daily social and cultural conditions in Algeria and the colonial system itself. Fanon conceived of the struggle for freedom and a new, postcolonial nation in the same way he approached the two-stage treatment of alienation in socialtherapy, that is, as a process first of destruction (the shock of colonization), then re-creation (revolution). Yet in a 1957 article for the review *Maroc médical* on the question of agitation, co-authored by one of his house officers, Slimane Asselah (who would be kidnapped that year by French paratroopers in his Algiers surgery and 'disappeared'), Fanon cast in doubt some of the guiding principles of socialtherapy and for the first time indicated a distance from Tosquelles. He questioned the notion that the Western model of hospital care, even in its most liberal configuration, could ever replace the outside world, and even if it did so it could not avoid the external relations of power.[6] Fanon realized that the psychiatric institution itself would need to be more comprehensively rebuilt, or potentially abandoned altogether, in order for a full psychic and cultural transformation to occur in a territory like Algeria, which appeared now to be unravelling in its very organization and operational structures. If mental pathology as experienced under – and caused by – colonialism constituted a 'veritable pathology of freedom', then armed revolution served as the treatment leading to a cure.

There were a few brief moments of respite for Fanon during this period of social convulsion, notably the arrival of a baby boy, named Olivier, in 1955. (Fanon arranged for Josie to give birth in Lyon in order to ensure that the child's nationality – French, born to French parents – would never be contested.) However, the joy was cut short by the news of his sister Gabrielle's passing in Le Lorrain, Martinique, aged just 33, during a premature labour. The pain was further aggravated by the knowledge that she did not receive adequate medical support from a doctor with whom she had earlier crossed swords. With her serious and commanding demeanour, Gabrielle had always inspired Fanon's respect, representing for him an ideal female figure. In a letter he wrote to his mother in which he poured out his profound grief, Fanon declared that Gabrielle was 'a simple, tender heart' whose death was 'grotesque'.[7]

The Blida region, where over 2,000 guerrillas were now operating in the mountainous areas and where outlawed *fellagas* (armed Algerian nationalists) were cutting off roads, had remained relatively quiet until the spring of 1956, after which it became increasingly volatile and insecure. There was an alarming rise in executions of nationalists and French reprisals on civilians. Meanwhile the workers' and students' strikes escalated in July, with nurses now joining the cause. Fanon had a sense of impending catastrophe. When the FLN restructured itself in August 1956 at the secretly held Congress of Soummam – the founding act of the modern Algerian state by which the FLN leadership established a Comité de Coordination et d'Exécution (CEE) and accorded full status to the ALN – he was still not integrated within it, his role restricted largely to local medical matters. However, in a sign of his increasing politicization, Fanon had already written a letter on 27 February 1956 to the French anarcho-communist author Daniel Guérin, hoping it might be published anonymously in the journal *France-Observateur* – to no avail, although Guérin did send parts of it to Sartre and the writer François Mauriac (again, to no effect). When this traditional means of drumming up left-liberal support failed, Fanon tried something different. In an undated and anonymous letter addressed simply to 'a Frenchman', he launched a blistering attack on 'you' – an individual positioned as a French friend who has suddenly declared his intention to leave Algeria. Holding him to account for ignoring the plight of the indigenous Arabs and *fellahs* (peasants) 'gorged with old biscuit which has to last all month', Fanon delivers damning home truths in spare and brutal language, intensified by grinding repetition and pointed reference to the massacre at Sétif:

> The shame of not having understood, of not having wanted to understand what was happening around you every day. For eight years you have been in this country. And no part of this enormous wound has held you back in any way. And no part of this enormous wound has pushed you in any way . . . All this leprosy on your body . . . I want my voice to be harsh . . . I want it to be torn through and through, I don't want it to be enticing, for I am speaking of man and his refusal, of the day-to-day rottenness of man, of his dreadful failure. I want you to tell.
> (*PRA* 56–8, *TAR* 48–50)

The 'Frenchman' was most likely Lacaton, who had not yet committed himself to the Algerian cause (he would, in fact, later be arrested and tortured for suspected collaboration with the FLN).[8] Yet by stating that he wanted his voice to be completely shredded, Fanon was perhaps also remonstrating with himself in a heart-to-heart dialogue of conscience. Certainly, this was a powerful and painfully honest use of the epistolary form by Fanon to discharge and channel pent-up, raw emotion.

By the middle of 1956 Fanon's double life was proving impossible. Terror was mounting on all sides, nurses were disappearing, medical supplies were depleted, and the daily toil and tumult of war were taking a heavy physical and emotional toll. He felt he was becoming

French troops sealing off the Casbah in Algiers on 27 May 1956.

less operationally effective in treating the psychic wounds of war
– for Fanon the bottom line. At the Congrès des Médecins Aliénistes
et Neurologistes de France et des Pays de Langue Française in
Bordeaux in September 1956, where he presented, alongside
Geronimi, the fruits of their culturally sensitive study of TATS,
Fanon made contact with the psychiatrist and longstanding anti-
colonalist Jean Ayme, who had supported Algerian independence
since 1945. Ayme introduced him in turn to the historian and
Trotskyist militant Pierre Broué. For the first time in public, Fanon
the clinician merged with Fanon the engaged intellectual – two
sides of the same cure.

Fanon returned from France in October just as the FLN set off
its first bombs in central Algiers, killing three people and injuring
dozens – an act of retaliation for a bombing by French police in
the Casbah when more than seventy people had died. The Battle
of Algiers – a period of intense urban guerrilla warfare led by the
FLN's military chief of the Autonomous Zone of Algiers, Saadi Yacef

– had now begun. Raoul Salan, who had authorized Fanon's war medal in 1945, was promoted to commander-in-chief of the French forces. A full-scale insurrection and inferno was on the cards, and the authorities were closely monitoring the hospital for signs of *fellagas*. By December the underground operations at Blida-Joinville had disintegrated. Some doctors were sacked or expelled; others departed voluntarily to escape imminent arrest. Nurses were seized and sent to camps, while others fled into the *maquis*. Fanon himself was now receiving death threats, and he and Lacaton were both at risk of arrest. The situation had reached a tipping point. Fearing his cover would be blown, Fanon chose to resign. In a very different second letter to a Frenchman, namely the Governor-General and Resident Minister Lacoste, he adopted both a highly personal and a political tone:

> If psychiatry is the medical technique that aims to enable man no longer to be a stranger to his environment, I owe it to myself to affirm that the Arab, permanently an alien in his own country, lives in a state of absolute depersonalization. What is the status of Algeria? A systematized dehumanization . . . A society that drives its members to desperate solutions is a non-viable society, a society to be replaced. (*PRA* 60–61, *TAR* 53)

Fanon had now finally spoken, and it was an utterly uncompromising statement of fact in the name, once more, of reason: 'No pseudo-national mystification can prevail against the requirement of reason . . . There comes a time when silence becomes dishonesty' (*PRA* 61, *TAR* 54). Explosive and accusatory while still eminently courteous, his resignation letter was tantamount to a declaration of war. It provoked Fanon's swift expulsion by means of prefectural decree. However, there was no Fanon Affair: the *Journal officiel* simply noted that, as of 1 February 1957, Dr Frantz Fanon had taken a leave of absence. In fact, he was expelled by means of a simple administrative act based more on an evaluation of his support for the doctors' strike than on his clandestine activities. (General Jacques Massu had just been handed overall control of French security in

Algeria, with orders to break all strikes.) The expulsion order probably saved his and his family's life: a bomb was thrown outside their home, although there were no casualties and no one claimed responsibility.

Before departing in late December, Fanon met, via Chaulet, the central figure in the war of liberation in Kabylia and the Algiers region, Abane Ramdane. He now agreed to put himself fully in the service of the FLN. In so doing Fanon sealed his fate with that of the Algerian people and effectively renounced his French citizenship. When the major French raid on Blida-Joinville finally occurred, in January 1957, some of the personnel were arrested, while others tried to cross to Tunisia on foot. Fanon had already escaped to France. The Blida experiment was over.

8

Public Acts of Provocation:
Fanon in Performance

After leaving Bordeaux in late September 1956, Fanon had headed
straight to Paris to attend the first International Congress of Black
Writers and Artists at the Sorbonne – a momentous three-day
gathering of Black artists and intellectuals organized by the
Senegalese writer and editor Alioune Diop, founder of *Présence
africaine.* Bringing together over sixty delegates representing
24 countries, the congress was structured around the idea of an
authentic African heritage and aimed, through panels and debates,
to engage a new, modern 'dialogue of civilizations' between Black
men of culture from the Caribbean, Africa and the United States.
Fanon was part of the Martinican delegation, along with Césaire,
Glissant and Louis T. Achille. Yet while this was a landmark event
in the history of Black internationalism, there were a number of
glaring gaps and omissions: the countries of the Maghreb were not
represented at all, and no mention was made of the situation in
Algeria. There were also no women speakers on the podium (a fact
publicly regretted by Richard Wright), even though the organizing
committee included Josephine Baker in an honorary role. In the
official group photograph of the delegates a sole female figure is
present: the wife of the Haitian writer and politician Jean Price-
Mars, seated between her husband and Diop in the front row. In
the same photograph Fanon is standing a little sheepishly in the
third row, second from left, his impassive face suggesting that other
things were on his mind (an FLN bomb network was at that very
moment being established in Algiers). Fanon was still relatively
unknown, of course, even in Black intellectual circles, and he was

not the top draw in Paris.¹ This was his first major non-medical speech, and the recording made of it constitutes the only complete extant record of him speaking (a slightly expanded version of the text was published in the June–November 1956 issue of *Présence africaine*, on which the English translation is based).²

The congress wished to highlight the growing importance of psychology and existential phenomenology as ways of understanding racism and colonization. Yet despite its title, the words *nègre* and *négritude* were seldom pronounced during proceedings. Moreover, most delegates refrained from endorsing explicit or radical anti-colonial positions. Senghor, who represented *négritude*'s canon, delivered a paper entitled 'The Laws of Negro-African Culture' in which he defined Negro-African civilization while foregrounding its complementarity with European civilization. Several delegates criticized this abstract, idealized image of African civilization, which appeared entirely disconnected from colonial matters. Césaire argued in 'Culture and Colonization' that the question of Black culture was completely unintelligible without reference to colonization, and that it was vital to address

Attendees of the first International Congress of Black Writers and Artists at the Sorbonne, Paris, in September 1956. Fanon is in the third row, second from left.

colonized people as agents and creators.[3] However, only Fanon's contribution, entitled 'Racism and Culture', dealt directly with the complex historical and cultural processes of racism and the often paradoxical evolution of Black consciousness. More a lecture, it marked a major turning point in Fanon's career as an engaged public intellectual. It was a dazzling and dynamic performance showcasing his remarkable facility with language and encapsulating his polemical and declamatory style – at once vehement, systematic and unstoppable.

Fanon was the last to speak in the morning session on Thursday, 20 September. After taking care to compliment the previous speaker, the Sierra Leonean academic Davidson Nicol ('a hard act to follow', he repeated somewhat archly), he launched straight into his argument with no formulaic conference niceties. His opening salvo set the uncompromising tone: 'The unilaterally decreed normative value of certain cultures deserves our careful attention. One of the paradoxes immediately encountered is the rebound of egocentric, sociocentric definitions' (*PRA* 39, *TAR* 31). He presented anti-Black racism as embedded within the very fabric and values of European culture, but again discounted essentialist, racialized thinking as central to Black liberation struggle: nothing from a racist culture can engender liberatory racial thinking. He ripped into the lack of reflection by the proponents of *négritude* on their own psychological mechanisms as colonial elites. Fanon's chief targets, however, were the European colonial governments who attempted to prove that they did not hold racist prejudices while continuing to colonize foreign lands and export their own cultures as the superior choice. He saw a logical impossibility in someone abandoning racist ideas while also participating in a system or institution (such as colonialism) built upon racism, which entailed 'the destruction of cultural values, of ways of life' (*PRA* 41, *TAR* 33), including the devalorizing of language, clothing and skills. (As Cherki later recognized, Fanon was a genuine cultural anthropologist who militated in favour of a culture in movement and the need to open up points of cultural reference by underlining cultural differences, as opposed to the ethnopsychiatrist who relies on a

kind of culturalism and prescribes the return to a static identity.[4])
Fanon's implicit model of colonization and racism was Algeria,
to which he made only veiled allusion by referring to Kabylia
and the Kabyle *djema'as* (governing councils) appointed by the
French authorities. He had to be careful about referring to the
independence struggle, of course, as he was surely being monitored
and could not openly declare his support of the FLN. His most
blatant invocation of Algeria was his use of the North African Arab
term *razzia* (surprise attack), a tactic that the French forces were
now employing. That the situation in Algeria could be cured only
by the destruction of the colonial system is made transparent in
Fanon's conclusion when he refers to 'a people that undertakes
a liberation': no non-Western nation can enter into dialogue
with the West until unconditional liberation has been achieved.

Fanon's method of argumentation in 'Racism and Culture' is at
once dialectical and historical, proceeding via discrete stages. He
covers all bases, ranging freely across multiple fields and approaches
(historical account, socio-psychological examination, clinical study
of collective neurosis) while simultaneously flexing his rhetorical
muscle with signature moves of repetition and inversion to tell the
simple but hard truths about the colonizer and colonized. 'The
racist in a culture with racism is therefore normal' (*PRA* 48, *TAR* 40),
he explains, while 'what he [the inferiorized] does is in fact to
cultivate culture [*une culture de la culture*]' (*PRA* 49, *TAR* 41). Fanon
moves from the dry sociological ('The social constellation, the
cultural whole, are deeply modified by the existence of racism';
PRA 44, *TAR* 36) to the visceral ('the occupant's spasmed [*spasmé*]
and rigid culture'; *PRA* 52, *TAR* 24), punctuating his analysis with
absolutes and abstract universals ('a psychological datum that is
part of the texture of History and of Truth'; *PRA* 49, *TAR* 41) as well
as with concrete turns of expression stretching the bounds of the
literary and scientific – for example, his suggestion that culture
'can't be put between slide and cover glass', as under a microscope
(*PRA* 49, *TAR* 41). We are brought into contact with a quicksilver
intelligence in the act of fleshing out and formulating concepts,
moving metaphorically in and around ideas, perpetually nuancing

and qualifying them ethically ('anti-Jewish prejudice is no different from anti-Negro prejudice . . . There are no degrees of prejudice,' he insists (*PRA* 49, *TAR* 41)). The result is an exciting and daring verbal *métissage* incorporating technical words that often come back to the body: 'encysted', 'amputation', 'cortical integration', 'mummified'/'mummification', 'axiological activity', 'sclerose'/'sclerosed'. Some of the dynamism of the original French, often configured in short, apodictic sentences with no main verb, is unfortunately lost in translation, and some words remain unaccounted for in the published French and English versions. Missing, for example, is the second instance of the verb *cracher* (to spit) to describe 'the oppressed' in the clause: 'sa façon de s'asseoir, de se reposer, de cracher, de rire, de se divertir' ('his [the native person's] way of setting down, of resting, of spitting, of laughing, of enjoying himself').[5] Fanon no doubt added the repetition on the day for onomatopoeic effect, stacking up five infinitives in a row in a form of sonic overload. Another peak of intensity through accumulation is reached in his ominous summing up: 'This culture, abandoned, sloughed off, rejected, despised, becomes for the inferiorized an object of passionate attachment' (*PRA* 49, *TAR* 41).

Fanon's oral delivery is rapid, animated and relentless, the shifting modulations and pulsations of his voice ushering different perspectives and subject positions ('us', 'them', 'you') as he fires off volleys of words and slices nimbly through cultural metaphors for racism even as he has recourse to them. He understood instinctively that, by mastering discourse, one controls the situation in which one is operating, and he is always in forward momentum here in a compelling synthesis of intellect and emotion. He soars, as if unassailably, in his cadences, interrupted by spontaneous applause on at least four occasions – enough for him to catch his breath, recharge and aim still higher. His urgent, driving verbal rhythms and bravura play with rhetorical language to form part of the polemical effect and function of his political engagement, as if the performance were itself enacting the liberatory struggle. It makes this and many other of his public interventions feel more like a rallying call to arms.

Portrait of Fanon during the 1950s.

For Fanon, public speaking extended the writing process, which could be an all-consuming, heady experience as he engaged with what he called the 'magic' of words and language in its very materiality: 'Words have for me a charge. I am unable to escape the *bite* of a word, the *vertigo* of a question mark' (emphasis added), he explained to Jeanson.[6] He aimed to decolonize discourse by opening it up viscerally at the physical level of the word – the *skin* of language – in order to, as he claimed to Jeanson, 'move' his reader, 'irrationally, almost sensually', adding in a clear allusion to Césaire that he wished to 'sink beneath the stupefying lava of words that have the colour of quivering flesh'.[7] Such sensorial language, although at times courting opacity, produced immediate sensations out of which an original, not merely conceptual, reflection might reveal itself in a flash of illumination. This instantiates Fanon's apocalyptic idea that racism and culture can start to be disentangled only when culture itself, as currently formed, becomes unintelligible and effectively disintegrates: 'The end of race prejudice', he declares at the end, 'begins with a sudden incomprehension' (*PRA* 51, *TAR* 44).

'Racism and Culture' may be compared stylistically in this regard with Fanon's articles for *Esprit*, notably 'The "North African Syndrome"', which proceeds initially in standard scientific terms while deploying striking vocabulary such as 'pseudo-invalid', 'scotomizing' and 'thingify'. Working so intimately in the flesh of language stimulates a continuous flow of new formations in the argument – of advances, detours and flanking manoeuvres – as Fanon searches for the right angle of attack. He rehearses different critical positions and perspectives before staging dramatic dialogues with projected others, both implicit and explicit. The essay eventually adopts an incriminatory style, climaxing in a furious face-off between 'I' and a second-person 'You' (the indigenous French physician), whereby the first-person narrator assesses 'Your' attitudes to a third-person ('Mohammed') whom 'You' (which shifts suddenly from the polite '*vous*' form to the familiar '*tu*') have systematized: 'Your solution, sir? Don't push me too far. Don't force me to tell you [*vous*] what you ought to know, sir. If YOU [TU] do not reclaim the man who is before you, how can I assume that you reclaim the man that is in you?' (*PRA* 25, *TAR* 16; original emphasis).

In the later 'West Indians and Africans' of 1955, which addresses the presuppositions of race and racialized thinking and is historically framed by his wartime experience, in particular his recollection of repeated exchanges with West African soldiers about the actual 'Blackness' of 'quasi-metropolitan' Antilleans, Fanon feels his way methodically towards an incontrovertible position. He again inveighs against the delusions of *négritude* and its nostalgic projection of Africa, voicing doubts about an undifferentiated Black people and Blackness as an identity, an idea he derides by force of repetition: 'not only the colour black was invested with value, but fiction black, ideal black, black in the absolute, primitive black, the Negro' (*PRA*, 35, *TAR* 24). Nothing in Fanon's writing is left to chance: all is working in unison, confidently and efficiently, in the interests of a penetrating new analysis designed to admonish and unsettle the reader. A cultural consideration of irony, for instance, crystallizes into a scathing paradox: 'In Europe irony protects against existential anguish, in Martinique it protects against the awareness of *négritude*' (*PRA* 28, *TAR* 19). The article culminates with an incendiary juxtaposition of two devalorized extremes: 'the great white error' of colonialism and 'the great black mirage' of *négritude* thinking that led the Antillean to plunge into 'the great "black hole"' (*PRA* 36, *TAR* 27).

In each of these electric verbal performances, the sense of a ceaseless cascade of words, of surging energy and resolve through rhetorical flourishes and poetic amplification, creates the impression that Fanon is staging a virtual assault on his audience. Jeanson employed the term 'surgissement' (upsurge), in his preface to *Peau noire*,[8] but more appropriate perhaps is 'insurgency', which Jeff Sacks has proposed to describe how the subject in Fanon reiterates the philosophical and linguistic forms it wishes to contest. This double gesture succeeds in *overflowing* the privileged categories in European colonial disciplines for understanding and practising sociality. As Sacks attests, Fanon offers his reader and listener 'a practice of struggle'.[9]

Fanon's breathlessly dense and defiantly difficult intervention in Paris overwhelmed his audience and reduced it to silence. Mission accomplished. Yet the silence persisted: the speech was barely discussed and generally ignored by the invited press, along with Fanon's name. Only much later did *Les Temps modernes* hail its heartfelt plea for solidarity and fraternity and Fanon's potent call for a postcolonial future. Despite the muted response, however, Fanon was formally elected to the executive committee of the institutional off-shoot of *Présence africaine*, the Société Africaine de Culture. More fundamentally, he had articulated the question that would henceforth consume him: how to attain first a national consciousness and then proceed to a universal understanding, such that all societies and cultures might come together and be reconciled? The closing words of 'Racism and Culture' promote a respect for reciprocal relational difference: 'The two cultures [that is, of occupier and occupied] can affront each other, enrich each other' (*PRA* 52, *TAR* 44). The challenge of how to arrive at this stage of universal recognition is one to which Fanon would devote the rest of his career.

9

My Name is Ibrahim:
Exile in Tunis

When Fanon returned on his own to Paris in January 1957,
followed soon after by Josie and Olivier, he found himself at a
major crossroads in his life. He had been banished from Algeria,
the country to which he had now wholly committed himself, and
was exiled in France, a country he could not identify with any
more, for in his eyes he was no longer French. The family laid
low in an apartment provided by Jean Ayme at the psychiatric
hospital of Clermont-de-l'Oise, north of Paris. Since Fanon could
not expect any remuneration from Governor-General Lacoste
and thus had little money, Ayme supported him financially
during these difficult first weeks. When Josie briefly departed,
entrusting Olivier to Ayme's wife, Fanon was left at home
alone, reading into the early hours the documents of the early
Communist International in Ayme's library. (Lenin's thesis that
the capitalist stage of economic development was not inevitable
in the colonies made for instructive reading.) It felt like a period
of premature semi-retirement. Recharge, rewire, re-engage: this
was Fanon's automatic reflex. But how to start all over again?

Ayme advised Fanon not to get caught up in politics and to
return to psychiatry, but for Fanon now, psychic life was always
already a political formation. Manville, in whose apartment at
Porte de Champerret in Paris he subsequently stayed for a month,
counselled him a little differently, encouraging him to focus on the
movement for independence in the Antilles. Instead, Fanon met up
again with Jeanson, who was now establishing a network that would
shortly include *porteurs de valises*, who transported money raised

by Algerians living in France and destined for Swiss bank accounts, thus providing the means to get Fanon out of France. Fanon's view of Jeanson's efforts and those of his fellow French sympathizers could be haughtily dismissive: he saw them as mere intermediaries who had little immediate impact on the Algerian struggle for decolonization. This was symptomatic of Fanon's general scorn for the debased French Left, who were more preoccupied with the abortive Hungarian Revolution in 1956 than with the crisis in Algeria. That said, Fanon was happy enough to avail himself of Jeanson's support (he could be mercenary when needs dictated).

During this period Fanon also had a brief meeting with Daniel Guérin, who supported the Messalist line on the grounds that it enjoyed support from urban proletarian workers and peasants in both Algeria and France. According to Guérin, Fanon's hatred of Messali verged on the fanatical, yet he continued to regard the FLN as the only way forward because he knew Messali would never break entirely with the French.[1] He then met at last with Salah Louanchi, leader of *wilaya* VII (that is, the French Federation of the FLN), who offered to help him get to Tunis, where the FLN was organizing itself politically and medically. This was duly arranged and, in what would be the last safe passage organized by Louanchi (he and the entire leadership of the French Federation were arrested at the end of February in Paris), Fanon travelled alone through Switzerland by car to Rome, landing in early March in Tunis, just 130 kilometres (80 mi.) from the Algerian border. Josie and Olivier arrived shortly after. A new chapter in Fanon's life and career – another major turning-point in his journey of self-transformation – was about to begin.

The environment Fanon now found himself in was unique: following independence in 1956, Tunisia had become under its first president, Habib Bourguiba, the FLN's rearguard base: 150,000 Algerians resided there, both fighters and politicians. Before the Ligne Morice was constructed by the French in 1957 to prevent FLN guerrillas from entering Algeria via Tunisia and Morocco, border clashes between the ALN and French troops were frequent. In the capital, Tunis, which was fast establishing itself as a prosperous postcolonial city, the FLN operated like a virtual state-within-a-state. Another outpost existed in Tripoli, and the Conseil National de la Révolution Algérienne (CNRA) assembled in Cairo.

Fanon's reputation as a dynamic and pioneering psychiatrist had preceded him in Tunis, and he was already being sized up by the FLN as a useful addition to its communications network. His sheer force of personality and charisma succeeded in removing the usual impediment to integration within the FLN fold, namely a lack of Algerian nationality. The same man who, a few months earlier, had presented himself as a French doctor at neuropsychiatry conferences was now appointed to the FLN press office in central Tunis. Fanon quickly emerged as a public spokesman for the FLN, which calculated on using him to gain international credibility. The fact that he was unschooled in political theory and relatively uninformed made him all the more desirable for the position.

Fanon gained swift admission to the editorial staff of *Résistance algérienne*, the current official organ of the FLN. He was soon appearing as an Algerian delegate or representative in press conferences held in various African capitals. He eagerly assumed whatever role the Front called upon him to perform, representing the views of the FLN on its differences with Bourguiba, the prospects for negotiations with France, and the general elections in Algeria under the tutelage of the UN. During the summer of 1957 he would be summoned to Tétouan on the Moroccan coast to discuss the reorganization of the entire FLN press. His first public statement in Tunis, made during a press conference on 3 June 1957, was a response to the French discovery of a massacre in late May, in a hamlet outside Melouza in southern Kabylia, of around three hundred Muslim civilians who supported Messali's MNA. Fanon denounced the 'foul machinations over Melouza', insinuating that the French army was responsible, yet the FLN itself had carried out the atrocity.[2] Fanon could be diplomatic with the truth if operational success required it. If he harboured any misgivings about the FLN's tactics, he kept them private.

As the Front's media spokesman Fanon cut a striking if unusual figure: an elegant, high-powered, non-Muslim Black man in sharp

Fanon, flanked on his left by commander Kaci Hamaï, at the FLN press conference held in Tunis on 3 June 1957 to address the Melouza massacre.

European tweed suits who spoke no Arabic. About his scientific and intellectual interests he kept characteristically quiet: these were now relevant only to the extent they advanced the cause of the revolution. Yet Fanon felt vulnerable: he enjoyed no official position in the leadership and had an insider/outsider status among Algerian revolutionaries. His direct superior in charge of information, Abane Ramdane, was leader of the 'interior' forces and was increasingly perceived as a threat to the FLN's 'exterior' forces on the Tunisian side of the border (it was even rumoured he was creating a cult of personality). Like Ramdane, with whom he fraternized whenever they were both in Tunis, Fanon believed that peace negotiations could begin only after Algeria's independence had been secured and universally recognized. In this respect they formed a precarious hard-line faction within the FLN. But Ramdane was also a progressive who believed in a future Algerian state that promoted the 'primacy of citizenship over identities' (including that of religion) as the basis for a new polity. He would prove both an ally and mentor for Fanon.

During this period Fanon continued to practise as a psychiatrist, first at the Razi de la Manouba hospital, a public sector institution in the suburbs of Tunis (ironically, the clinic had been built in 1912 largely at the urging of Antoine Porot). It was a well-equipped hospital set in extensive grounds, and Fanon was given a spacious apartment in the administration block next to the entrance. Working under the assumed name of Dr Farès as one of a team of four consultants, he attempted to transform the limited provision of occupational therapy by introducing techniques of socialtherapy fine-tuned at Blida-Joinville, for example initiating a journal written by the patients called *La Raison*. Fanon was again operating squarely within the institutional network of psychiatry, for while in his political thinking he was an outlier on the fringes of the establishment (be it *Présence africaine* or the Left intelligentsia), he never worked on the periphery of the medical profession.

Fanon publicly expressed concern at the underlying limitations of a hospital like Manouba, arguing in one scientific article that 'In the neo-society, there are no inventions, there is no creative, innovative dynamic. There is no veritable shake-up, no crises. The institution remains the "corpse-like cement" of which [Marcel] Mauss speaks.'[3] In addition, Fanon did not get along with some of his Tunisian colleagues, who perceived him as overbearing and resented him for attempting to impose his demanding work ethos on others; they even referred to him openly as 'the Negro'. The fact that he also wished to reform the hospital setting did him no favours. The situation turned ugly when the director of the clinic, the conservative Tunisian doctor Taher Ben Soltane, became incensed that Fanon went over his head to request additional funding for occupational therapy directly from the health minister, using his personal contacts within the FLN and the Tunisian government. Soltane accused both Fanon and Charles Geronimi – his colleague from Blida-Joinville, who, along with Alice Cherki (now his wife), had followed Fanon to Tunis to join the FLN – of being Zionist spies for Israel. In Fanon's case this was no doubt because he had taken a clear stand against antisemitism in *Peau noire* and was close to Tunisian Jewish doctors. Fanon eventually prevailed and kept his post – evidence again of his determination to do whatever it took to achieve his goal (in this case money). However, he promptly moved out of the hospital accommodation to an apartment arranged by the FLN.

It was partly in reaction to the incident with Soltane that Fanon began work also at the Charles-Nicolle general hospital in Tunis, which had a neuropsychiatric unit. This was a well-advanced practice although it presented a daunting task: during the first few months Fanon had charge of over three hundred patients. Conflicts arose there too, but none that prevented the Tunisian health minister from unofficially tasking Fanon with a study of the reorganization of psychiatric institutions in Tunisia and the reform of different methods of treatment. It was at Charles-Nicolle that Fanon would now create and direct Africa's first psychiatric day clinic with the support of the local authorities. He had all the bars immediately removed from the windows, the wards were completely repainted, and patients were divided equally between men and women (in the case of the latter, a bedside ward for children was also made available). The Neuropsychiatric Day Centre was open six days of the week and had an open-door policy, which meant that patients left at night and returned the next morning, thereby remaining in contact with their families and, in some cases, the world of work. It was also easier in such a setting to treat semi-clandestine FLN fighters discreetly and quietly, for as at Blida-Joinville a number of Fanon's patients were traumatized veterans of the *maquis.* Accompanied by a Black Algerian nurse called Youssef, Fanon travelled every week with other doctors to a refugee camp at Kef, a small town 40 kilometres (25 mi.) from the frontier, where he attended to wounded ALN soldiers.

Fanon was assisted at Charles-Nicolle by Marie-Jeanne Manuellan, a field social worker and the only French woman working in the hospital. In his office – a small, empty box room without a door – he dictated to her his articles for typing, and she assiduously took notes while he performed his daily rounds. He would often refer to her solely by her function, that of recorder. However, typically, for someone who generously shared his knowledge and took particular satisfaction in educating others in the general interests of reform, Fanon also ended up training her medically, giving her first Freud and then Helene Deutsch to read. Manuellan would later write that, in doing so, Fanon had liberated her.[4]

Fanon wrote proudly about his work at Charles-Nicolle in a detailed two-part article in *La Tunisie médicale* (the second part on 'doctrinal considerations' was co-authored by Geronimi), where he outlined the advantages of a general hospital setting stripped of its carceral character.[5] He showed with graphs how a thousand patients had been admitted to the day centre, which enjoyed a high rate of success during its first sixteen months of operation (less than 1 per cent had to be committed to Manouba). As at Blida-Joinville, Fanon was attempting to create a society like that outside, in which patients could establish multiple social bonds, fill a variety of functions and take on different roles. He stressed again the sociogenic aspects of symptomatology: symptoms originated from a dialectic between the ego and the world that had been distorted (his preferred phrase 'pathology of freedom' to describe madness is twice used in the article), as well as from the internalization of social conflicts. His primary goal was therefore to 'consciousnessize' his patients' conflicts by enabling them to verbalize their symptoms and consolidate their sense of self. His therapeutic armoury included ECT, neuroleptics, hypnotherapy, narcotherapy, a variety of individual or group psychotherapies and even aspects of psychoanalysis. Fanon was typically pragmatic: he was interested less in abstract theoretical

Fanon with his medical team at the Charles-Nicolle hospital, Tunis, 1960.

Fanon teaching at
the Charles-Nicolle
hospital, Tunis,
c. 1959.

constructs or doctrinal purity than in what might actually work.
Along with Lucien Lévy, a Jewish communist doctor, he was involved
in clinical trials of a muscular relaxant called meprobamate, supplied
by a French pharmaceutical firm and eventually marketed as
Equanil.[6] He also recommended the use of drugs in disciplinary
territory annexed by psychoanalysis, notably for depression. Forms
of psychodrama were explored, along with visual art, involving in
one case a patient who was a practising artist (the drawings and
watercolours were later circulated by the FLN). The overall result
was a day centre that was low-cost and efficient and offered a
new holistic model of psychiatric care. It would in time lay the
groundwork for community-based mental health provision
in France.

Multi-Fanon Multitasking

Towards the end of 1957 Fanon started writing for *El Moudjahid* (The Warrior), the new FLN mouthpiece under the general editorship of Redha Malek that appeared every two weeks in French and Arabic versions. It preached mainly to the converted and was essentially a vehicle of propaganda, not so much gathering hard news as interpreting the information relayed by other news agencies, including *Le Monde*. This editorial work, mostly undertaken by Fanon at the FLN's offices at 24–26 rue Sadikia rather than at the journal's headquarters, now constituted his primary contribution to the elaboration of the official FLN line, both domestically and internationally. He pursued a cosmopolitan stance on international solidarity (in particular sub-Saharan Africa and Algerian unity) and helped turn *El Moudjahid* into a more complete paper commenting broadly on the social, economic and political aspects of the Algerian Revolution. All the material was unsigned and anonymous, in accordance with the FLN's policy that the individual was subservient to the collective. That said, Fanon's more polemical contributions were not hard to spot (Josie later detected 21 articles written by him, mostly single-authored, the rest collectively edited).

The articles for *El Moudjahid* fall well short of a history of this period: some events are prioritized while others are wholly ignored, such as de Gaulle's return to power in May 1958 and the birth of the Fifth Republic. Fanon's main target was his *bête noire*, the hypocritical French Left that had failed fully to support Algerian self-determination by citing FLN attacks on civilians, and which seemed less concerned with the shattered bodies and lives of an entire people than with French victims of torture and individual freedoms (high-profile testimonies – including *La Question* (1958) by Henri Alleg, editor of the left-wing *Alger-Républicain*, who was kidnapped and tortured in Algiers the year before – were now being made public). The PCF in particular was reluctant to oppose the war, voting in 1955 in favour of 'special powers' to suppress the rebellion, and it refused to condone the use of *porteurs de valises*. For Fanon, the complacent and morally vacuous French Left had effectively succumbed to the myth of 'l'Algérie française'. One especially vituperative three-part article he wrote on the topic in December 1957, entitled 'French Intellectuals and Democrats and the Algerian Revolution' (*PRA* 83–98, *TAR* 76–90), the second part of which was republished in *France-Observateur* with no indication of the author, set the cat among the pigeons in Paris. A French journalist speculated that it must have been written by someone with 'a taste for verbal outrages and psychological striptease'.[7] In fact, Fanon's unremitting diatribe, which castigated French democrats for their false neutrality and neocolonialist attitudes and concluded with a list of 'tasks' for the French Left, had already been watered down by the editors of *El Moudjahid*, who omitted Fanon's more inflammatory invective (including references to a 'perverted' France) before it went to press.

If Fanon's clinical and journalistic duties were not enough, he also accepted an invitation to teach social psychopathology at the University of Tunis. In his lectures from 1959 to 1960, which attracted not only sociology students but doctors, academics, Algerian militants and politicians, he tested out his evolving ideas about the relations between mental illness, war and violence, encompassing both the insane as alien and socially excluded, and the colonized as alienated from their own society. He also made radical observations on social and industrial psychology and how the workplace produces mental disorders, offering social diagnoses of the psychic effects of modern practices of control (records, files, time sheets, ID documents, surveillance) on different categories of worker. One of his students, the future Tunisian sociologist Lilia Bensalem, regarded Fanon as a captivating, if also forbidding, multi-personality: 'He [Fanon] was imperious, all the while being ready to listen to others, distant, passionate and fascinating; we asked him questions; but he rather tended to give monologues, to reflect on things out loud. His expressions were not only those of the doctor, but above all of the philosopher, the psychologist, the sociologist' (*AV* 517). As was his wont, Fanon took time after class to speak to the young students and even invited them to join him on his ward rounds at the clinic. The lectures were eventually cancelled, however, by order of the Tunisian government, and only a series of notes remain.[8]

Fanon was at the top of his game. All his current activities – doctor, clinical director, researcher, media representative, journalist, teacher – were coming together as if seamlessly in a total practice of engagement. According to his own criteria he was now most fulfilled because most effective operationally, even if his underlying desire to enter active combat on Algerian soil had been flatly refused by the ALN. On his own terms, too, he had resolved the ticklish question of identity previously based on the unitary, inferior status of the Black man imposed by colonial society, for he was fashioning a proliferation of roles and functions in postcolonial Tunisia that confounded the very notion of a fixed or circumscribed identity. As for daily life in Tunis, Fanon led a comfortable existence with Josie, who was now herself writing articles anonymously for the radical Francophone newspaper *L'Action tunisienne* and had been hired by Tunisian radio to host a literary programme. He was also developing a tender affection for his son, Olivier, even though he remained staunchly Martinican with regard to the division of labour in the family. He expected his wife and mother of his child to take care of all domestic matters, although he was always fully in favour of proper maternity leave. Joby later admitted that the dutiful Josie felt excluded from the tight, intimate bonds of the Fanon family and, because she never mastered Creole or learned to swim, often found herself on her own during his visits, when the two brothers amused themselves in the sea.[9]

More generally, Fanon cultivated a mainly European circle of friends and associates. He met French cultural figures and intellectuals passing through Tunis such as Raymond Aron and the actor-anarchist Jacques Charby, who collaborated on the production of educational material for child war orphans and distributed drawings by young children.[10] Fanon and Josie formed a close bond with Manuellan and her Armenian husband (an aid worker who, like Fanon, had fought in the Allied campaign in southern France during the Second World War), and the two couples got together regularly, playing the card game *belote* and engaging in long political discussions in which they criticized the Tunisian president, Habib Bourguiba, but never the FLN. Indeed, Manuellan's home in the nearby suburb of Mutuelleville became one of the few places where Fanon spoke about his early life in Martinique and played *biguines*. During one Christmas Eve party he drank and danced freely with Marie-Jeanne to the tune of Sidney Bechet's 'Petite Fleur', but when another guest took photographs he insisted the film be destroyed. Incriminating evidence of idle colonial pleasure? Proof he enjoyed the company of other women? Either way, he deemed it a bad look (it would not be the last time he attempted to suppress photographic evidence). Another mark of Fanon's discretion – of giving nothing away, to the point of *pudeur* – was his insistence on keeping his clothes on when they all went to the beach. Likewise at the cinema, he always sat in the front row to conceal his short-sightedness (he resigned himself to glasses only when speaking at large formal gatherings).

Tunis could still be a difficult, even hazardous space for Fanon, of course. He and Josie were a rare interracial couple in the North African context, and when he walked through the streets of the city he often felt hostility (according to local lore, the French spat on the Jews, who spat on the Arabs, who spat on the Blacks). For outside errands Youssef often went in his place, using a false passport under the name 'Farès', thus creating – in addition to Fanon's alter ego (Farès 1.0) – a doppelgänger (Farès 2.0). Among the few people Fanon felt he could fully trust within the FLN was the Berber and Marxist Omar Oussedik, although in public they resorted to whispering and code to guard against unwelcome attention, whether from French surveillance or rival FLN factions. In August 1958 Fanon obtained a new passport issued by the Tunisian consulate of the United Kingdom of Libya. It was valid for all countries and gave him yet another official identity: Omar Ibrahim Fanon, born 1925, place of birth Tunis, height 165 centimetres, black eyes, black hair, place of residence Tunis. It was a 'real false passport' because it was a genuine document issued under a false identity. Fanon was now Libyan! The alias, chosen for security reasons, exemplified the spirit of the revolutionary cause in which individual identity was

A studio portrait of
Fanon during the late
1950s.

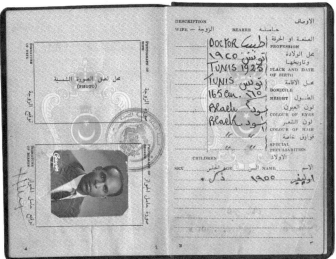

Fanon's diplomatic passport issued in Tunis, August 1958.

irrelevant, but for Fanon, of course, identity was already inherently mobile and contingent – there was no one 'Fanon'.

Fanon's first trip on his new passport was to Rome in September 1958, for reasons unknown but probably related to the establishment of the Gouvernement Provisoire de la République Algérienne (GPRA), declared in Cairo on 19 September 1958 with Ferhat Abbas as president. Yet just as Fanon was never a member of the Comité de Coordination et d'Exécution, FLN's ruling body, so he never held a position in this provisional government, which had been formed to internationalize the struggle on the diplomatic front and isolate France at the UN (GPRA diplomatic missions were now setting up around the world). The FLN itself was starting, however, to fracture and implode in a bloody internal power struggle. Although weakened within Algeria, where the *wilayas* were becoming fragmented, it was expanding elsewhere. The external leadership wished to bolster the so-called 'army of the frontiers', and figures like Ramdane, who represented the interior campaign, had long been an obstacle. Colonel Houari Boumédienne began a rise to power that led to 'Opération Bleuite', a series of purges carried out in 1958 and 1959 by Colonel Amirouche on FLN cadres falsely accused of collaborating with the French in Kabylia (*wilaya* III). A year after the Melouza massacre, on 29 May 1958, *El Moudjahid*'s front page announced that Ramdane had died 'on the field of honour'. In fact, Ramdane had already been dead for five months, strangled by 'comrades' in a villa on the Algeria–Morocco border. Fanon knew the truth of his friend's murder but stayed silent for his own safety. He may also have been aware that his name now figured on an FLN hitlist in the advent of any threats to its leadership.

The shocking death of Ramdane, whom Fanon regarded as Algeria's true leader for his vision of a republic free of clans, had a profound emotional impact on him. He felt he had his friend's death on his conscience. Could he have saved Ramdane by preventing him from going to Morocco? Certainly, Fanon's naivety regarding the scale of conspiratorial policies had been cruelly exposed. His torment was aggravated when he found he had to endorse a wholly false version of Ramdane's death in the pages of *El Moudjahid*. It was a

Front cover of *El Moudjahid*, 29 May 1958, announcing the news of Ramdane's death.

further punch to the gut. At the same time Fanon's official status in Tunis was downgraded when the information minister for the GPRA, M'Hamed Yazid, a smooth operator with strong links to the French Left, assumed overall control of communications and displaced him as the FLN's media spokesman in Tunis. Fanon loved Algeria more than anything – after all, he had relinquished so much for Algeria, even a strict adherence to historical fact – and his dedication to the cause of national freedom remained absolute. But where next could he securely go to pursue the revolution he so passionately believed in? His only answer for the moment was to return to the calmer and more reliable territory of the written page.

10

Lifting the Veil/Preaching Revolution

L'An v de la révolution algérienne (literally, Year 5 of the Algerian Revolution), published by François Maspero in 1959 and later in translation under the title *Studies in a Dying Colonialism* (shortened to *A Dying Colonialism* when republished by Grove Press in 1967), was Fanon's contribution to the *littérature de combat*. It was a militant book designed to articulate clearly and accessibly the cause of Algerian independence and to detail the remarkable mutations now emerging in Algerian society and the national consciousness after five years of revolutionary struggle, when Algerians were transforming from colonial objects into autonomous subjects. 'Year 5' also alludes to the French revolutionary calendar, expressing Fanon's belief that a new historical era had begun on 1 November 1954. The decisive turning points in Algerian society may have partly mirrored Fanon's own transformation as an activist and revolutionary, yet the book was not intended as a personal or self-reflexive account: this was squarely a sociological study (called as much in later editions by Maspero) devoted to promoting the effects of social revolution that transgressed the restrictive physical and mental boundaries of the colonial order. Buoyed by revolutionary enthusiasm and optimism, Fanon offers here an illuminating account of how national liberation struggles can break up the colonized nations' old strata of culture and allow for the renewal of forms of expression and the rebirth of the imagination, in the process producing more equal relations between people freed from their inferiority complex and ultimately a new humanity – or, as he puts it, 'a new Algerian society from top to bottom'

(*AV* 87, *ADC* 101). The 'I' of *Peau noire* has now morphed into 'we Algerians', and, for the first time in his written work, Fanon foregrounds the work of women – an exceptional move in the political circles in which he was moving. (When the Algerian writer Assia Djebar arrived in Tunis in 1958, she found that within the GPRA only Fanon was interested in any writing that did not simply glorify revolutionary fighters.) Yet *L'An v* also shows Fanon continually wrestling with the values of tradition and centuries-old customs (derided by the colonialist oppressors as 'primitive') and their place within the revolutionary process.

Fanon had only brief periods of time to dedicate to the book and wrote it speedily over a matter of weeks in the spring of 1959, drawing on notes and drafts from Blida-Joinville as well as extensive discussions with Geronimi. The haste perhaps accounts for a much less honed literary and rhetorical style than in *Peau noire* and the odd factual error (Fanon presents the day of 'fraternization' in 1958, when Algerians were shepherded in Algiers to declare 'l'Algérie française', as 13 May – three days too early). It was to Manuellan rather than Josie that Fanon dictated the manuscript, from seven o'clock to nine o'clock in the morning, before his daily consultations. She described the experience as 'the ceremony of the Book': 'His sentences flowed all by themselves to the rhythm of his steps around the room. He never sat down. He had no notes in his hand.'[1] The ten-page introductory preface (dated July 1959), which he wrote himself because the various people he had approached (Césaire, Memmi, Ferhat Abbas) declined, was not included in the first edition by Maspero, no doubt because of its often highly belligerent tone (it contained sweeping statements such as 'the most hallucinatory war that any people has ever waged to smash colonial aggression'; *AV* 5, *ADC* 23).[2] In fact, the book was based directly on Fanon's daily encounters with fighters, nurses and local people in their daily lives at Blida and in Tunis, and offers one of his most detailed and sensitive accounts of the horrors and traumas of the war and of the destruction of Algerian culture. As Cherki observes, this is very deliberately a work about the common man and woman rather than the personalities and actions of revolutionary elites.[3] Moreover, Fanon is always focused on the creativity and movement of lived collective experience at this exciting stage of national awakening. He impresses upon his reader that '*we* have wrenched the Algerian man from a centuries-old and implacable impression. *We* have risen to our feet and *we* are now moving forward . . . *We* do not believe there exists anywhere a force capable of standing in *our* way' (*AV* 14, *ADC* 32–3; emphasis added).

Organized in chapters buttressed by 'annexes' to maximize the impression of objective, scientific case studies, *L'An v* explores systematically five principal axes of transformation within Algerian society and tradition. Most patent is the radio, which for so long had been an organ of repression (specifically Radio-Alger) but which, as the chapter 'This is the Voice of Algeria' reveals, was now a channel of communication for the revolution and a source of unity for the people. Fanon examines the collective struggle by Algerians to listen to the pirate radio broadcasts of the FLN on the newly created radio station transmitting from Morocco, La Voix de l'Algérie Libre et Combattante, reclaiming their own voice in the process. What interests Fanon is less the actual content of the broadcasts than the fact that they are disrupted by static and scrambled by the French jamming the airwaves. Each dispersed listener had therefore to reassemble and actively interpret a message by sharing captured snippets in conversation with their fellow countrymen and women, with the result that 'Every Algerian . . . broadcast and transmitted the new language' (*AV* 72, *ADC* 87). The resulting new forms of social interaction constituted what Nigel C. Gibson neatly calls a 'wireless democracy', for 'the militant now had to listen to the people (to the subaltern who had become audible)'.[4]

'The Algerian Family' demonstrates how the revolution altered the way Algerians thought about families as homogenous and monolithic. Fanon considers in turn different kinds of family relation to show that the traditional hierarchy of the father and first son taking up patriarchal leadership roles no longer operated during the war since brothers and sisters were thrown together in military units, with the result that the leadership structure was flattened out and increasingly merit-based. Men and women lived together in barracks and could be involved as a married couple in ways inconceivable before, but which should still be described as 'Algerian' because born of shared national struggle. Fanon writes further that female society was changing owing to its organic solidarity with the revolution and because (employing deliberately dramatic language) 'the Algerian woman penetrates a little further into the flesh of the Revolution' (*AV* 36, *ADC* 54).

In 'Medicine and Colonialism', in which Fanon contends that France used access to medicine as part of its war against colonized people already deeply suspicious of Europeanized doctors, his method is again to delineate different modalities (the consultation, medical surveillance, the native doctor, the European doctor). The emphasis is characteristically on the body, of both the revolutionary and the nation: 'Once the body of the nation begins to live again in a coherent and dynamic way, everything becomes possible' (*AV* 133, *ADC* 144–5). Yet he also challenges official nationalist discourse by resisting any false universalizing turns to nativism: the defiant behaviours of the colonized must be viewed as a consequence of colonial structures and not as an immutable feature of the 'native psychology' or the 'basic personality' (*AV* 133, *ADC* 145).

In another routine attack by Fanon on the pusillanimous French Left, 'The European Minority of Algeria' (published also separately in *Les Temps modernes* in June 1959) exposes the European intellectuals who had taken up the cause of the settler. Acknowledging that the various ethnic groups and communities in Algeria had a different level of investment in society because the institutions were built along racial lines, he provides a taxonomy of Europeans in Algeria, starting with the Jews and their place in the colonial hierarchy: some work for the police but many are involved in the struggle and may be viewed as the 'eyes and ears of the revolution'. In the case of the Algerian settlers, Fanon typically cautions the need for nuance: there are some good apples who have provided support and refuge. The third category are the doctors and pharmacists caring clandestinely for the FLN and ALN and helping to keep Algerian prisoners safe. He salutes those 'European democrats' who have refused to divulge any information under torture before asserting that everyone living in Algeria and fighting for national liberation is *de facto* Algerian, and that, in the independent, multi-ethnic Algeria of tomorrow, every Algerian will be able to choose whether they wish to assume or reject Algerian citizenship. The chapter is supported by testimony from Geronimi (the Algerians treat me like a brother, he enthuses) and a statement from a former French policeman who now professes to be Algerian. Together the two men exemplify Fanon's idea that in the process of revolution everyone is (re)born Algerian, whatever their background.

The defining chapter of *L'An v*, which continues to attract the most critical attention, is the first, 'Algeria Unveiled', about the status of Algerian women. The force of the original title, 'L'Algérie se dévoile', employing a feminine noun and an active reflexive verb, is lost in the English translation with its passive construction. Rather than being 'unveiled' by another, Algeria is embodied here as an active female subject who chooses to *unveil herself*. Equating the nation with womanhood, the title carries a powerful irony in that, as Fanon will show, it means one thing for the colonizer and another for the women engaged in revolutionary struggle.

In by now familiar fashion, Fanon approaches the evolution of the veil in Algeria – and its change in cultural meaning on both a symbolic and instrumental level – as a series of historical phases. First was the settlers' self-serving attempt to 'emancipate Muslim women' by pressurizing them to Europeanize themselves by removing their veils, construed by the French as a symbol of humiliation and segregation. However, this only served to make the veil more popular and a means of resistance: 'The veil was worn because tradition demanded a rigid separation of the sexes, but also because the occupier *was bent on unveiling Algeria*' (*AV* 45, *ADC* 63; original emphasis). Second was the taking up by Algerian women of the colonizers' call for modernization and 're-monetization' by abandoning the veil and circulating in the colonial city 'like sound currency' (*AV* 24, *ADC* 42). Yet the French failed to perceive that the Algerians, 'radically transformed into [European women], poised and unconstrained' (*AV* 39, *ADC* 57), had entered circulation as counterfeits. The removal of the veil allowed female partisans to fight back against the colonizers and become part of the military wing of the revolution. Even women not actively integrated into the struggle formed the habit of abandoning the veil. The French were unable to grasp that, under their very eyes, 'grenades' and 'activity report[s]' (*AV* 32, *ADC* 50) were being smuggled. Third was the moment when, after their deception had been exposed by 'certain militant women' speaking under torture (*AV* 43, *ADC* 61), the activists reassumed the veil but only as a further means for passing undetected: now submissive-looking women were carrying their arsenal underneath their veils. The varied and dynamic role of Algerian women, from transporting bombs to giving shelter to combatants, is traced by Fanon in admiring detail, for they turned the veil against its original meaning. Positioned as passive within their cultural tradition, they used the veil actively to hide bombs, remaining perfectly visible yet unreadable to the colonizers' gaze.

Women ALN fighters in combat gear loading firearms during the Algerian War of Independence, *c*. 1955.

'Algeria unveiled' is thus a metaphor for what the European imaginary cannot see: the secret 'truth' staring it in the face – that is, the revolutionary unveiling of a nation recreating itself through armed revolution.

Fanon employs the phenomenological concept of the corporeal schema from *Peau noire* to formalize a new dialectics of the body and the world resulting in subjectivity. As Khalfa highlights, if in removing their veil to infiltrate the colonizer's society the women's former corporeal schema is distorted in a potentially traumatic event of self-exposure, nevertheless it becomes possible for them to invent a new one and for the structure of traditional society to be transformed, this time from the inside.[5] Fanon's belief is that an Algerian woman, through the very act of (re)claiming her body differently, can invent 'new dimensions for her body, new means of muscular control'. Yet to create for herself 'an attitude of unveiled-woman-outside' and 'relearn' her body, she must literally walk a fine line: 'She must overcome all timidity, all awkwardness (for she must pass for a European), and at the same time be careful not to overdo it, not to attract notice to herself' (*AV* 41, *ADC* 59).

This process of freeing one's body from the colonizer's controlling gaze in order to establish a new subjective and transformative relation to the world is once again for Fanon a matter of invention and performance, owing to the unique possibilities provided by the struggle to adopt a new persona. The Algerian woman holding a gun has to imagine her own identifying object, because who she is becoming as she assumes that identity is not a 'figure' confined by known conventions of femininity. Indeed, her strategic use of the way in which she dresses, veils or unveils herself challenges the normal connections between self-presentation and who she must be according to custom. She is clearly nothing like the European woman when she carries a grenade in her bag, ready to use, if required, in acts of political terrorism. Indeed, the apparent mimicry of the Western woman may not involve psychic identification at all if played out consciously for the revolution. Fanon is celebrating here a woman's ability to organize and 'master' her lived experience in line with national sovereignty, and he appears in genuine awe of female guerrillas who are able to pass stealthily into enemy territory again and again to deliver safely their message to its destination.

Yet there are moments in Fanon's account when he lays himself open to the charge of fetishizing the body of the (un)veiled Algerian woman who comes to represent national identity in an Algerian republic that does not yet exist. For he approaches the veil from a distinctly unreconstructed male perspective, even rehearsing White European male fantasies and colonial stereotypes that fit within a visual iconographic tradition of exoticism and Orientalism, in which the veil acts as a perverse attraction for the (heterosexual) European man, and in which its removal or tearing is tantamount to – or metaphor for – rape. Already in the second paragraph of the chapter Fanon presents Algerian women in the manner of a European tourist bewildered by their striking beauty. He appears at times spellbound by the visual spectacle he is depicting, whether it is the unveiled woman walking 'stark naked' into the European city, where he wishes to see the body beneath the veil, or the maturing body of young Algerian women. Indeed, he writes with flagrant fascination that 'The body of the young Algerian woman, in traditional society, is revealed to her by its coming to maturity [*la nubilité*] and by the veil. The veil covers the body and disciplines it, tempers it, at the very time when it experiences its phase of greatest effervescence. The veil protects, reassures, isolates' (*AV* 40–41, *ADC* 58–9). Conversely, removing the veil creates for the Algerian woman a sense of 'disintegration': 'she has the impression of her body being cut up into bits, put adrift . . . the unveiled body seems to escape, to dissolve' (*AV* 41, *ADC* 59). This is on account of the explosion of desires suddenly generated by her subjectivity that neither she nor men of whatever background (Arab or European) can control, which therefore poses a threat to Fanon's standard of mastery required for the achievement of subjectivity.

'Algeria Unveiled' is immediately followed by a short appendix (a short article from May 1957 entitled 'Women in the Revolution') intended to prove that Algerian women were always regarded as central to the struggle. It is premised on Fanon's claim that in 1955 the FLN started to recruit and involve women directly (at first only older, married women). Yet Fanon's highly sophisticated account of the instrumentalizing of the veil, which consciously idealizes the role of female activists at the expense of a more complete picture of the longer-term changes for women, arguably downplays their importance, for they not only carried bombs but planted them. Moreover, there is little real acknowledgement of the veil's religious implications as a symbol of Islam, so eager is Fanon to prove that this object of tradition has lost its taboo character during the revolution because removed from its original cultural context. This oversight is perhaps all the more surprising in view of Fanon's celebration of the quasi-religious aspect of the new society. The Algerian people may be physically dispersed and separated because they are forced to take refuge in Tunisia and Morocco, but, in a typical Fanon inversion, they are forging through suffering and trauma a new unity: 'a spiritual community which constitutes the most solid bastion of the Algerian Revolution' (*av* 105, *adc* 120). Fanon verges at times here on the evangelical in his messianic invocation of a new dawn. 'The Algerian nation is no longer in a future heaven' (*av* 12, *adc* 30), he preaches, solemnizing revolution almost as a form of divine retribution effected by the will of the people. He extols 'This community in action, renovated and free of any psychological, emotional, or legal subjection' (*av* 167, *adc* 179).

Fanon returns to this spiritual dimension in his short two-page conclusion, in which he underlines his view that the revolution has already passed the point of no return. It is also more fundamental and far-reaching than the mere fact of national liberation, since it is a transformative moment of enduring change: 'The Revolution in depth, the true one, precisely because it changes man and renews society, has reached an advanced stage. This oxygen which creates and shapes a new humanity – this, too, is the Algerian Revolution' (*av* 168, *adc* 181). The powerful vocabulary of cultural dynamism employed by Fanon to herald a new age in formation – words like 'upheaval' (*bouleversement*), 'spontaneous', blossoming' (*épanouissement*), 'mutation' and 'effervescence' – contrasts with the deadening language used to dismiss the colonizer's misguided entrenchment ('solidity', 'crushing of the Algerian revolution', 'asphyxiation', 'death through exhaustion'). The 'spiritual' conditions of this 'New Man', new society and new humanity are established through material struggle and constitute thus a separate category from organized religion, which, Fanon argues, can be complicit with colonial oppression and neocolonial manipulation and divide the peoples of newly decolonized countries. Hence, while not denying Islam's capacity to act as a progressive force against colonialism, he considers that conventional forms of religion have no real place in the revolution. In fact, Fanon consistently paid little attention to – and seriously underestimated – the reassertion of Islam in Algeria's independence struggle. As Adam Shatz observes, Fanon was proposing 'a nationalism of the will, rather than of ethnicity or religion', yet what 'he failed (or refused) to see was that influential sectors of the nationalist movement were keen to reinforce religious conservatism'.[6] Left-wing officials in the FLN, such as the future historian Mohammed Harbi, voiced frustration that *L'An v'*s affirmation of the veil effectively allowed Algerian patriarchy to claim Fanon as 'a mouthpiece who presented its behaviour as progressive'.[7]

The new revolutionary dawn had still fully to arrive, of course. Yet on a personal level Fanon appears to have attained in *L'An v* a perfect fusion of the roles of engaged writer, clinician and political activist. Six months after its appearance, the French government ordered all copies of the book to be banned and forbade further publication, thereby cementing its radical status. Although it remains Fanon's least-cited work, French reviewers at the time hailed its first-hand knowledge of the Algerian situation from within. Fanon had finally secured an audience among those for whom his book was explicitly intended, namely the small but growing number of progressives in the French Left, such as Sartre, whose *Anti-Semite and Jew* is artfully referenced.

11
Accra, Pan-Africanism
and the Southern Front

In December 1958, travelling with a transit visa issued by the British
Embassy in Tunis, Fanon flew via Rome to Nigeria and from there to
newly independent Ghana to participate in the inaugural All African
People's Conference (AAPC) in Accra, attended by delegates from 25
countries. It was his first visit to sub-Saharan Africa and the first
time he represented the FLN in an international arena. It was also
his first time speaking to a pan-African forum, and the connections
he made between the Algerian Revolution and the broader context
of African anti-colonial struggle, including the recognition shared
by many of the possibility of a federation of African states, were
decisive for his future thinking. The congress brought together the
leading figures of African independence in a public show of political
strength and purpose, including the charismatic Ghanaian prime
minister Kwame Nkrumah; Patrice Lumumba of the Mouvement
National Congolais (MNC); Álvaro Holden Roberto (under the
alias Rui Ventura) of Angola; Tom Mboya, general secretary of the
Kenya Federation of Labour (KFL); and Félix-Roland Moumié, leader
of the Union des Populations du Cameroun (UPC) and a fellow
doctor, with whom Fanon quickly struck up a close friendship.

Fanon's impassioned speech on national liberation was another
searing performance. Gripping both sides of the lectern, he leaned
forward in his pale blue suit to create what the Algerian-born
French writer Jean Daniel Bensaïd later described as a kind of
emotional communion in the audience, despite the fact that no
simultaneous English translation was available.[1] He made the
solemn case for armed resistance as a necessary last resort in the

Fanon speaking at the All African People's Conference, Accra, December 1958.

struggle for freedom. Such a bold commitment to violence went directly against the declared spirit of the panel and the congress more generally: the socialist Nkrumah, for instance, was a pacifist who promoted non-violent struggle and 'positive action'.[2] However, the speech was greeted with wild applause and completely shifted the tone and direction of the occasion. Fanon was jubilant: Algeria was now leading the way in revolutionary progress and serving as a model for the rest of Africa. Nkrumah, who would become a trusted friend, even intimated that he would soon recognize the GPRA (in time he would also support Fanon's stance on violent retaliation to achieve freedom for Africans). In one of the two pieces he wrote on the congress for *El Moudjahid*, entitled 'Algeria in Accra', Fanon declared that 'the great figures of the Algerian Revolution – [Ahmed] Ben Bella, [Larbi] Ben M'Hidi, Djamila Bouhired – have become a part of the epic of Africa' (*PRA* 168, *TAR* 150). Neither of his accounts, however, mentioned that he also met with Césaire, Glissant and Paul Niger to discuss the formation of an organization advocating for political autonomy for the French Antilles and uniting Martinicans, Guadeloupeans and Guyanese. This was because the political situation in Martinique remained of only minor concern for Fanon. (After Glissant and Niger returned to Paris and recruited Manville and other prominent Antilleans to the organization, it was quickly dissolved by French presidential decree, and all members of its leadership were barred from the Antilles.)

A few months later, in late March 1959, Fanon attended the second Congress of Black Writers and Artists in Rome, in which he now formed part of the Antillean delegation. As usual, Josie was on hand to oversee the practical arrangements, just as Manuellan did during the medical rounds at Charles-Nicolle (this was all the more necessary in Italy, where Fanon was reminded of the insidious obstacles of everyday European racism). Fanon was becoming increasingly internationalist and wished to make the Algerian struggle part of a global movement for liberation. However, as with the first congress, the focus of the gathering at the Italian Institute for Africa was more cultural than political, and Fanon found himself the only speaker from the Maghreb. He kept a low profile and was barely visible (in one official small group photograph, which includes among others Glissant, a figure appearing to be Fanon hovers elusively in the background). His speech, 'The Reciprocal Basis of National Cultures and the Struggles for Liberation', was not welcomed by some and struck a discordant note, for now he was speaking about the nation-state in general terms rather than about African countries specifically. Yet for Fanon any authentic culture was by definition a national culture, hence any attempt to miss out the national stage of development, which paved the way for the eventual creation of international alliances between nation-states, would prove an error. Fanon was sharing here his still evolving thoughts about nationalism: while critical of making it the privileged form of Third World struggle, he supported national cultural movements in the wider revolutionary struggle in Africa. The speech was received with a mixture of broad agreement and blatant disapproval, but it confirmed Fanon's emerging political stature and influence.

All was looking promising for the FLN on the international and pan-African front, and Fanon was helping to make it happen. He was viewed by many not only as in the vanguard of the movement for freedom in Africa but as the primary lynchpin for bridging the gap between Arab North Africa and Black sub-Saharan Africa. The FLN's seemingly unstoppable momentum led to Tunis hosting the Second All African People's Conference in January 1960. Opened by President Bourguiba, it examined the positive changes that had occurred across the continent in the previous few years. Fanon confidently requested on behalf of the Algerian delegation, and as proof of Africa's 'political choice', the establishment of an international body of African volunteers whom Algeria would train in the methods of 'subversive warfare' (a scheme first mooted at the Accra conference). Fanon would have to wait a long time, however, to receive a clear response.

Fanon's participation in the FLN's international mission was not without danger. A number of assassination attempts were made on his life, the first in June 1959 when he was on the Algeria–Morocco border treating wounded soldiers. During a trip to a village, the jeep he was being driven in suddenly skidded out of control after hitting a landmine – either that or the vehicle had been sabotaged. He was thrown out of the car onto his back. Josie rushed immediately to be with him in the nearby hospital at Oujda, headquarters of the Western Frontier army, but such were his

In transit: Fanon walking up a ship's gangway preceded by FLN representative Mouloud Gaïd and followed by Redha Malek, editor of *El Moudjahid*, date unknown.

Fanon in Tunis with Ahmed Boumendjel (seated to his left), head of information of the FLN and director of *El Moudjahid*, n.d.

injuries (twelve vertebral fractures, a damaged sphincter, his lower body paralysed) that he was transported by plane to Rome in early July for medical treatment. It was here that he narrowly escaped a second assassination in a bizarre series of events involving the FLN delegate to Rome, Taïeb Boulahrouf. Boulahrouf's car, which was taking him to Ciampino Airport to meet Fanon, exploded en route. Fanon was travelling with a Moroccan passport and a changed name but was informed the next day that certain newspapers were reporting the recovery, in the clinic where he was being treated, of a 'senior Algerian politician' to whom the explosion appeared connected. Noticing that the number of his first-floor room had been inadvertently given in one article, he asked to be transferred to a third-floor room. During the night two armed individuals broke into the clinic, entered the room originally assigned to Fanon and, finding it empty, fled. Both this and the first attempt on Fanon's life were most probably perpetrated by La Main Rouge, a terrorist organization operated by French foreign intelligence.

Fanon's stay in the clinic at Rome lasted until the beginning of August, after which he spent a period of convalescence at

Hammamet, on the east Tunisian coast. The Fanon who resumed
duties at Charles-Nicolle and *El Moudjahid* was fully reinvigorated
and, true to form, excitedly mapping out new prospects for militant
activism. His wish for a new venture was eventually answered
in February 1960 when he was suddenly appointed permanent
representative (or Head of Mission) of the GPRA in Accra – a
singular achievement for someone who was neither Algerian nor
Muslim. He departed first for Cairo, the location of the GPRA's
Ministry of Foreign Affairs, where he spent two weeks consulting
archives and discussing the basis of an African policy in preparation
for his new role. He arrived in Accra in March. The embassy was
little more than a small apartment, and as a roving ambassador for
a self-proclaimed provisional government he enjoyed few privileges.
He was in many ways stateless: relying on a Libyan passport, he
still had to obtain tourist visas before he could travel and was
often obliged to stay in hotels and borrowed rooms. Fanon would
generally grow to like Accra, where he performed no medical or
psychiatric work, yet his limited English did not allow him to
experience fully the political and social life of the capital. It didn't
help that Josie quickly caught malaria and had to return to Tunis
with Olivier, leaving Fanon on his own and often at a loose end –
the chance, if nothing else, to acquire a taste for gin and tonic.

As Algerian ambassador to Ghana, Fanon focused on three
main issues: a pan-African campaign to recruit volunteers to fight
in Algeria, part of his burgeoning idea of an African Legion; the
establishment of a southern flank in Mali for channelling these
recruits to the front; and the armed struggle in Angola and events
in the Congo. Contradicting his earlier views on the need for national
cultures, he now sought to promote African unity as a prelude to
the creation of a United States of Africa, with Accra the headquarters
of African liberation south of the Sahara. After all, as he declared
during his 1958 speech in Accra, an Algerian could not be a true
Algerian if he did not feel in his core the unspeakable tragedy also
unfolding in the two Rhodesias and Angola. His ultimate objective
was to provide the Third World with a genuine internationalism –
a commonly shared ideal that had remained at the level of vague

formulations since it was initially proposed in April 1955 at the Bandung Conference, the first major meeting of newly independent Asian and African states. For Fanon, Africa was a unity forged ideologically through shared anti-colonial struggle. In an article published in *El Moudjahid* in January 1960 entitled 'Unity and Effective Solidarity are the Conditions for African Liberation' (*PRA* 189–93, *TAR* 170–73), in which he asserted the need for liberation movements across the continent to maintain neutrality during the Cold War, Fanon stressed that 'inter-African solidarity must be a solidarity of fact, a solidarity of action, a solidarity concrete in men, in equipment, in money' (*PRA* 192, *TAR* 173).

The year 1960 was pivotal for national independence across Africa. The fledgling states were now negotiating with ex-metropolises and the two superpowers while weighing up the options of an African form of socialism. Fanon attended a succession of conferences as an official representative of Algeria: the International Conference for Peace and Security in Africa in Accra in April, where, speaking in a quiet and sober voice, he gave another unsparing speech about the regrettable necessity of armed violence as the 'only solution' for the Algerian people owing to the inhuman violence displayed by French forces in Algiers;[3] the Afro-Asian Peoples' Solidarity Conference in Conakry in April; the Third Conference of Independent African states at Addis Ababa in June; and in August the Pan-African Congress at Léopoldville (now Kinshasa), convened by Lumumba as prime minister, who was at loggerheads with President Joseph Kasavubu (the Congo was teetering between acting on Lumumba's anti-colonial ideals and accepting the return offensive of Belgian colonialism).[4] At the Conakry conference, opened by Guinea's first president, Ahmed Sékou Touré, Fanon gave a soaring performance in which he appeared almost to break down as he scorned de Gaulle's newly fledged (and short-lived) 'community' of African states as another kind of French imperialism, while also denouncing African countries including Côte d'Ivoire and Senegal whose 'negative neutralism' had led them to sign compromised defence and economic treaties with France. At such assemblies Fanon's natural authority allowed him to make positive, albeit intermittent, contact with numerous African leaders of independent countries and independence movements. However, for all the official rhetoric of unity, only a few newly independent African states were ready to sign up to his brainchild of an African Legion. In the case of Ghana, which became a republic in July 1960, the country was taken up more with domestic matters in its tangled struggle to emerge from underdevelopment. Even the FLN did not consider pan-African unity a priority.

The fact is that, while Fanon was an outstanding mobilizer and propagandist, he was not a natural diplomat. His ingrained life-or-death approach and restive impatience for results that worked so brilliantly in the hospital setting, where it was only ever a matter of improving and saving life, could become complicated and even counter-productive in the political sphere, where careful negotiation, strategic alliances and even machinations were required. He possessed little political savvy and could be easily swayed by strong, single-minded personalities. For example, he placed faith and allegiance in dynamic revolutionary figures such as Sékou Touré

Fanon and M'Hamed Yazid representing the FLN and Algeria at the Pan-African Congress, Léopoldville, 27 August 1960.

Fanon with Holden Roberto (centre) and the Yugoslav journalist Zdravko Pečar in Tunis, unknown date.

in Guinea and the Angolan guerrilla leader Holden Roberto, who both appeared to share his pan-African vision. Touré would ironically turn Guinea into a one-party state and become an autocrat. In the case of Roberto, whom Fanon regarded as a champion of the rural masses, Fanon's naivety took a more baleful turn. He went excitedly to Lisbon to visit Roberto and others involved in the Angolan struggle for independence, and, at his behest, the GPRA gave support to Roberto's new Union of the Peoples of Angola (UPA). Overreaching himself (he had little real knowledge of Angola), Fanon rushed headlong into discussions about setting up a new front on either the Moroccan or Tunisian border with Algeria where the FLN could train a small group of UPA cadres as part of a continent-wide struggle. However, Roberto was actually a tribal chief who had cultivated ties with the CIA since 1955. Angola would soon be consumed by civil war.

Although the life of a jobbing diplomat plane-hopping across the continent was a tiring and often frustrating business for Fanon, on a personal level it afforded him opportunities for recreation. At the Conakry conference he found himself leading an Algerian delegation to an evening of entertainment laid on by the Guinean government that included bare-breasted women dancing. Fanon was not prudish but would probably not have witnessed such a spectacle before, certainly not in Algeria. While acknowledging his acute embarrassment, the open display of naked breasts wholly bedazzled him, to the point he would later fixate on them in his memory of the event.[5] Just as Fanon could turn on his immense charm when required, so too, in the right company, he could be frolicsome. Later that August, at the World Assembly of Youth (WAY) in Accra, he met a fresh generation of young protesters, including the American sociologist Immanuel Wallerstein and the young American activist and WAY organizer Elaine Klein (later Mokhtefi). In her memoirs of the period Mokhtefi wrote of her heady encounter with Fanon, with whom she smoked French *gauloises* forbidden by the FLN: 'One night, Fanon and I went dancing. A Ghanaian photographer focused his camera on us. Frantz caught him on the edge of the dance floor and warned him to destroy the photo (it appeared nevertheless in an Accra newspaper a few days later).'[6] Fanon, of course, never wrote about such gallivanting, but it no doubt inspired him to champion the political value of dance. He later explained giddily in *Les Damnés* that 'The circle of the dance is a permissive circle: it protects and permits. At certain times on certain days, men and women come together at a given place, and there, under the solemn eye of the tribe, fling themselves into a seemingly unorganized pantomime . . . There are no limits' (*DT* 58, *WE* 44). Mokhtefi herself credits Fanon for advising her always to be autonomous and to pursue her own goals on her own terms.[7]

Boys' Own Adventures in the Desert

While the general project of pan-Africanism continued to preoccupy Fanon, he was also entertaining the possibility of opening up a new southern front through Mali and the Algerian Sahara to help relieve the beleaguered fighters of *wilayas* V and VI. Arms were already travelling that route, leaving the port of Conakry and wending their way through Mali to Tamanrasset and Aïn Salah on the backs of

camels and men. Fanon had visited Bamako at the beginning
of the summer of 1960 and held propitious talks with Mali's new
president, Modibo Keïta, and other key figures such as Madeira
Keïta, minister of the interior. Now, in October, he set off on a
dangerous reconnaissance mission to Mali approved by the GPRA
to find new military routes and supply lines for transporting arms
and munitions across the Sahara from Mali into Algeria. Fanon was
finally doing practical work in the field – the complete man of action
for the FLN he had always envisioned – and he was accompanied by
an eight-man commando led by Commandant Chawki, a major in
the ALN. Travelling under the name of 'Doctor Omar', he flew with
Chawki from Accra to Monrovia, where they planned to pick up
a connecting flight to Conakry. On arriving, however, they were
informed that the plane was full and that they would have to wait
for an Air France flight the following day. Suspecting a trap by
French intelligence, they drove by jeep 2,000 kilometres (1,240 mi.)
into Mali, with Fanon kitted up in Arab attire as camouflage. They
were right to do so: the plane, they later learned, had been diverted
to Abidjan in Côte d'Ivoire and searched by French forces. (Fanon
was convinced the plot had been orchestrated with the tacit
approval of Félix Houphouët-Boigny, Côte d'Ivoire's first president.)

The drive to Mali took Fanon and his team to Gao, Tessalit and
Bouressa on the Algerian frontier, where they made contact with
Malian nomads. During the journey Fanon kept a logbook so he
could later make a full report.[8] Although precise dates and distances
are lacking, it is a fascinating document that presents Fanon in prime
operational mode, writing adroitly about the numbers of men and
weapons required for the massive operations being planned and
airing intimate thoughts in a manner at once intellectual, clinical
and emotional. He records his feelings of being intoxicated by the
vast and changing landscape (tropical forest, savannah, desert).
In a rapid and at times rhapsodic narrative style, Fanon gives free
rein to his lyrical side, writing breathlessly about the stunning
sunsets that 'turned the robe of heaven a bright violet' (*PRA* 206,
TAR 185). He waxes ecstatically: 'That is the real Africa, the Africa
that we had to let loose in the continental furrow, in the continental

direction. The Africa that we had to guide, mobilize, launch on the offensive. This Africa to come' (*PRA* 199, *TAR* 179). At times Fanon's steely optimism of the will slips into wild triumphalism. Employing a rhetoric of conquest not too far removed from that of colonialism, he deemed that Africa needed the help of foreign revolutionaries with energy and vision. It was his mission, he states grandiloquently, to 'Stir up the Saharan population, infiltrate to the Algerian high plateaus . . . Subdue the desert, deny it, assemble Africa, create the continent . . . hurl a continent against the last ramparts of colonial power' (*PRA* 207, *TAR* 180–81). This is Fanon's idealizing revolutionary rhetoric at its most undiluted.

A crucial element of Fanon's excitement is that the adventure was experienced entirely with men, as if he were reliving the close intimacy he had shared with his brothers growing up. Chawki in particular, a 'small, lean [man], with the implacable eyes of an old maquis fighter' (*PRA* 202, *TAR* 181), becomes a focus of admiration verging on awe. 'I constantly marvel at the intelligence and clarity of his ideas' (*PRA* 202, *TAR* 181), Fanon swoons, adding matter-of-factly that he shared a bed with Chawki. Fanon had already acknowledged sharing a bed briefly with the paramedic and former ALN soldier Amar Boukri at a base on the Algeria–Morocco border the previous year, but that experience had not elicited such a powerful reaction. Now, Fanon appears dewy-eyed and spellbound by Algerian masculinity and its potent combination of physical strength and sagacity.

The suggestive, homoerotic force of Fanon's intense identification with Algerian masculinity and idealization of male contact raises the question of sublimated homosexual desire. The queer theorist Terry Goldie contends that, in his bonding moment with Chawki, Fanon is positively exploring the homoerotic possibilities of homosociality.[9] Fanon, he asserts, finds true liberation in the achievement of subjectivity through male homosocial relations in which female participation is effectively elided: the Black man 'must seize his freedom and be free to act, to choose. This freedom demands mastering one's life, one's desires, one's position in society.'[10] Here Goldie is directly citing Françoise Vergès, who argues that Fanon

Fanon (second from right) with members of the ALN at Oujda on the Algeria–Morocco border, unknown date.

recovers subjectivity through an act of will by consistently disavowing Martinique and constructing instead a family romance around Algeria, where he locates his symbolic ancestry.[11] That is, he denies Creole filiation – the emasculated Martinican father (a colonial construction) and violated mother – in order to make the FLN's virile fighters his symbolic father and brothers. Indeed, later in *Les Damnés* Fanon writes that the new militant, having formerly sublimated his energies in dreams of 'muscular prowess' and 'aggression' (*DT* 53, *WE* 40), retrieves the 'tonicity of muscles' (*DT* 55, *WE* 41) and feels his 'forgotten muscular tensions' unclenching and his imagination developing (*DT* 229, *WE* 194). Matthieu Renault shows further that national liberation is intimately linked in Fanon to an erotics of liberation, since muscular tension is an erotic tension and the colonized individual's hypersensitivity a form of sensuality.[12] Fanon speaks of 'libido works' and an 'overexcited affectivity' (the force of the original French, 'en érection' (*DT* 57), is lost in the English translation by the phrase 'sensitive emotionalism' (*WE* 44)). There is 'an erotic delight' to be had 'in the muscular deflation of the crisis' (*DT* 57). Counter-violence is thus also a *counter-libido*.[13]

Such full-bodied erotic moments are far more generous and mutually affirmative than the phobic lurchings of *Peau noire*, in which Fanon approaches homosexuality in regressive, pathological terms as a form of psychosis. For as equally problematic for Fanon as the Black man's neurotic desire for White women is the notion of the Black homosexual, who, he claims – astonishingly – simply does not exist in Martinique. Or rather, Fanon first admits then immediately disavows that there is any homosexuality in Martinique, referring in a long footnote to the presence of *commères* ('godmothers'), the queer cross-dressers only too visible in Fort-de-France during the 1940s (*PN* 146, *BS* 180). By implying that Black male homosexuality exists only for the perverse enjoyment of the degenerate White man ('There are men who go to "houses" in order to be beaten up by Negroes: passive homosexuals who insist upon black partners'; *PN* 143, *BS* 177), Fanon is really saying that the Black homosexual exists solely as a victim of the slave mentality: 'real' Black men are heterosexual and healthy. Put differently, the Black homosexual is for Fanon a phobic creation of the White gaze, a screen onto which White fantasies of fear and guilt can be projected in the form of perverted desires. Fanon is influenced here by Chester Himes's 1945 novel *If He Hollers Let Him Go*, about the destiny of its hero, Bob, in which the White woman's fear of being raped represents a desire to be raped. Her male equivalent is a repressed homosexual. Such ambivalence of psychic identification is explained troublingly by Fanon thus: 'the Negrophobic woman is in fact nothing but a putative sexual partner – just as the Negrophobic man is a repressed homosexual' (*PN* 127, *BS* 156). Fanon's definition of phobia as a matter of sexual fear and revulsion becomes self-inscribed when he later confesses: 'I have never been able, without revulsion, to hear a *man* say of another man: "He is sensual"' (*PN* 163, *BS* 201; original emphasis). Writing elsewhere in *Peau noire* of colonial society's scapegoating of Black people and Jews, Fanon plainly acknowledges his recourse to homophobic tropes: 'Fault, Guilt, refusal of guilt, paranoia: one is back in homosexual fantasy' (*PN* 148, *BS* 183).

Without suggesting that identifying with Algerian masculinity allowed Fanon to come to terms with – and meet – a psychosexual need or urge (an interpretation robustly disputed by Joby and Manville), the episode of homoeroticism in the logbook reveals that just being in such close physical company with other men is already for him a form of liberation.[14] It may at the same time express an underlying wish to progress beyond the necessarily complex inequalities and asymmetries of desire altogether, in a liberating move away from the individual to the collective that engenders a new form of human intersubjectivity – a chaste, secular, democratizing, homosocial love 'in the company of Man, in the company of all men' (*DT* 304, *WE* 254).

In military terms the reconnaissance mission ultimately proved fruitless. The FLN remained unwilling to commit resources to the southern Sahara, in part because it could not rely on the support of the various desert peoples. The trip had also left Fanon utterly exhausted and emaciated, even if on his return to Accra he immediately set to work on a contribution to an English-language bulletin produced by the GPRA's mission in Ghana, entitled 'The Stooges of Imperialism'. Fanon had reason to be worried about his

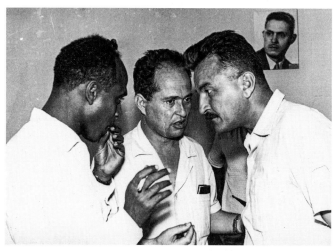

Fanon discussing strategy with Omar Oussedik (centre) and the Yugoslav journalist Zdravko Pečar (under a portrait of Algerian trade unionist Aïssat Idir) at Fanon's apartment in Tunis, 1960.

health: an examination by a doctor in Accra raised the possibility
of leukaemia. Once back in Tunis in December he took further
tests that confirmed a diagnosis of myeloid leukaemia, that is, a
high level of white corpuscles (leucocytes). In the most optimistic
clinical hypothesis he had two or three years to live, although more
realistically only a matter of months, since his skin was already
discolouring with a greenish cast. One photograph of Fanon from
around this period, taken during a meeting with fellow militants
(including Abdelaziz Bouteflika, the future president of Algeria),
captures him sitting with shirt unbuttoned on a couch looking
oddly unkempt and discernibly haggard. When he revealed the
devastating news of his condition to the Manuellans, Fanon sought
typically to downplay it, even laughing it off as something he would
fight with his brain alone (he never brought up the subject again).[15]

Just days before this shocking news Fanon had announced to
Manuellan that he was ready to dictate a new book. It would be
called *D'Alger au Cap* (From Algiers to the Cape) and draw on his
travels in Africa.[16] Yet the illness was already taking over. In the
following weeks he suffered a retinal haemorrhage, and there was
now a real danger that the cancer would spread to his spleen and
liver. He was flown to Russia early the following spring and treated
for several weeks in a clinic outside Moscow with the chemotherapy
drug Myleran. It was not a cure in itself and had many unpleasant
side effects (nausea, vomiting, diarrhoea), but it relieved some
of the symptoms. The Russian doctors advised Fanon that only
specialists in America were capable of providing treatment to
counteract a rapid decline. They also advised him to conduct a
'clinical' existence – that is, to consider himself already dead in
order to survive. Fanon could not countenance going to the United
States, 'the nation of lynchers', and returned to Tunis in April.
He now had another brief window of opportunity to write as the
cancer went into remission. He even proposed to the leaders of the
GPRA that he be sent as a permanent representative to Cuba, where
the mesmerizing revolutionary leader Fidel Castro was now prime
minister – a proposal given short shrift in light of his poor health.
In fact, Fanon was put to good use during these months, delivering

a political course for ALN officers stationed on the Algeria–Tunisia border. It demanded a great expenditure of energy, but Fanon was driven by the imperative to contribute to the political formation of those 'peasant-warrior-philosophers' of the interior whom he regarded as the true avant-garde of the revolutionary process.[17]

There was a sense of time running out fast, both personally and politically. Fanon even underwent the trauma of losing his sight for two weeks on his return to Tunis. His growing despair was aggravated by the passing of two of his closest allies, Moumié and Lumumba. Moumié was poisoned in Geneva in November 1960 by an agent of the French secret services, a month after he and Fanon had shared a flight from Accra to Libya. Fanon was devastated by the news, for he had seen in Moumié a kindred spirit who embodied the essence of revolution, at once 'aggressive, violent, full of anger, in love with his country, hating cowards . . . Austere, hard, incorruptible' (*PRA* 200, *TAR* 180). As for Lumumba, in September he was overthrown in a Belgian-sponsored coup, a prelude to his bloody assassination in January 1961 at the age of just 35. Fanon regarded Lumumba's death as one of the great African tragedies: although observing neutrality in the Cold War while pursuing a nationalist and pan-African agenda, he had relied fatally on the UN (viewed by Fanon in monolithic terms as a tool of Western governments) in a forlorn attempt to secure independence without violence and revolution. Fanon blamed himself for not having done more to disabuse Lumumba of his misplaced faith in the UN, although during the Léopoldville conference in August he and Omar Oussedik (now GPRA ambassador to Guinea) had tried persistently to persuade Lumumba to renounce his position as prime minister in order to reconsolidate his party.[18] Fanon was overcome with grief and returned briefly to Accra. As energy continued to seep out of his body, it seemed now that he had finally run out of options.

12

Down to the Wire:
The Damned Reborn

On 7 April 1961 Fanon wrote to Maspero that his health had improved and that he was engaged on a new book different from the one he had originally proposed. Parts of it were dictated in haste to Manuellan (but also to Cherki and Abdelaziz Bouteflika) from a mattress on the floor of the family's new, still bare Tunis flat, where he lay gaunt and feverish. Claude Lanzmann, a member of the editorial board of *Les Temps modernes* who met Fanon in Tunis in early 1961, remembers him as 'already so suffused with death that it gave his every word the power both of prophecy and of the last words of a dying man'.[1] The body of the text was progressing in inverse proportion to the regression of his own ailing body. As his condition deteriorated, Fanon composed frantically with few notes, creating a nightmarish picture of colonial Algeria that merged into his impressions of the independent African states he had visited. The almost-complete draft of the work entitled *Les Damnés de la terre* (literally, The Damned of the Earth) was prepared in about ten weeks. A final chapter was written at a reduced pace and finally sent, together with the conclusion, to Maspero in late July, with the instruction to consider the text 'whole and definitive'. It was the cue also for Fanon to get back in circulation, renewing contacts and intervening during the episode of Ferhat Abbas's dismissal as president of the GPRA. He started to prepare for the upcoming meeting in August of the CNRA, an organization to which, typically, he did not belong.

Les Damnés is another unique, heteroclite, multi-perspectival Fanon text, encompassing political analysis and military strategy, literary-cultural reflection and psychiatric inquiry, including clinical case studies. The title is taken from the end of the 1945 poem 'Sales Nègres' (Dirty Negroes) by the Haitian poet Jacques Roumain, a defiant expression of West Indian *négritude* as revolt. The title of the English translation, *The Wretched of the Earth*, which recalls the first verse of the Communist anthem the 'Internationale' ('Arise ye wretched of the earth'), does not fully convey the poetic potential of 'the damned', a theme Fanon had already announced in *Peau noire* ('Not yet white, no longer wholly black, I was damned'; *PN* 112, *BS* 138). Yet *Les Damnés* reads very differently, as a practical handbook for revolutionary consciousness and (post-)revolutionary action, including postcolonial governance. Its primary target audience were militants and those in revolt, in particular the valiant soldiers of the ALN from largely rural and peasant backgrounds whom Fanon so admired. By turns euphoric and apocalyptic in mood, it offers a searing indictment of settler colonialism, a critical account of the military struggle against colonialism and a radically democratic vision of total emancipation. Fanon reveals here what is possible when the social and political order undergoes profound fracturing of the scale experienced in Algeria, but also the imminent risks and dangers to the new postcolony. A measure of the book's universalism is the fact that, aside from a brief allusion to the OAS's assassination of the mayor of a French town (Évian) in March 1961, there are few specific references to the current situation in Algeria, where freedom fighters were now entering a deadly endgame with France.

The first chapter, 'Concerning Violence' (a slightly revised version of an article published in *Les Temps modernes*, with supplementary references to contemporary events in Martinique and the Adolf Eichmann trial taking place in Israel), begins with the portentous words: 'decolonization is always a violent phenomenon' (*DT* 39, *WE* 27). Fanon's central argument is that, because the colonial world is indelibly marked by violence (it is violence in its natural state), it calls for a liberatory counter-violence, or what he calls, adding a new term to his lexicon, 'la praxis absolue' ('absolute line of action'; *DT* 82, *WE* 67), that is, an irrevocable act of commitment binding the people together. Much of the chapter's early discussion is devoted to showing the nature of colonial violence caused by the 'primitive' Manichean ideology of colonialism, including a graphic critique of the compartmentalized colonial city – a world 'of segregated and barbed wire entanglements' (*DT* 41, *WE* 30) – which divides the colonial world into racialized zones of obscenely contrasting wealth. Within the native population Fanon identifies three modalities: the urban worker, the intellectual (compromised because a go-between with the colonizer and operating in the colonizer's language), and the lumpenproletariat lying outside the system of urban colonial and anti-colonial struggle (subsistence farmers, peasants, slum dwellers and others). The latter are 'the damned of the earth' – not just the sociologically wretched and poor but 'the pimps, the hooligans, the unemployed and the petty criminals . . . all the hopeless dregs of humanity' (*DT* 126, *WE* 103–4). Fanon charts the process of indigenous people rising up in collective armed revolt to reclaim both their land and dignity by externalizing their internalized violence and destroying their inferiority complex. The shock of resubjectifying has an immediate cleansing and cathartic force, disalienating their consciousness through the exultant idea of a 'common cause, of a national destiny and of a collective history' (*DT* 90, *WE* 73). Fanon prioritizes the damned as privileged subjects because their reparative transformation into revolutionary subjects is the most complete and pure. Condemned as outcasts, they are driven, as Miguel Mellino notes, 'by something that transcends them: a universal mission, the moral duty to redeem humanity'.[2] This inspires the prophetic, Christian tones of Fanon's latent messianism, for he presents the case for a purificatory, even divine violence, heralding the advent of a new 'spiritual' community 'evocative of a confraternity, a church, or a mystical body of belief' (*DT* 128, *WE* 106). Apocalyptic, 'spontaneous' violence is an 'absolute beginning' or '*tabula rasa*' (*DT* 39, *WE* 27) – a total and complete substitution that restores history to the people, brings invention into existence, and ensures 'the first . . . shall be the last' (a quote from the New Testament, Matthew 20:16).

Fanon bases many of his ideas on what he had personally witnessed in Algeria, including the fact that interpersonal violence

An assembly of ALN soldiers during the Algerian War of Independence, 1958.

among indigenous men stirred by dreams of possession and tribal warfare had been positively channelled into the common fight. Yet in customary fashion he also goes it alone theoretically: his romantic, utopian claims about the revolutionary force of the peasantry and his unshakeable belief in the power of the masses (the 'great organism' of violence) to determine the flow of history, which lead him to dismiss the notion of elite revolutionary structures and the role of the 'pampered' working class, were at odds with the views of the FLN leadership. They also contradicted reality, since the peasant population had never been a major force in Algeria, and vast numbers of rural dwellers were now exiled in internment camps. As Neil Lazarus suggests, it was more a question of wish-fulfilment on Fanon's part and a projection of his totalizing will onto the people.[3]

Much of the rest of *Les Damnés* is taken up with the nitty-gritty of the transition period of independence and the complexities of postcolonial society, culture and politics. Fanon attends to the grave threats posed by the opportunistic national bourgeoisie and intelligentsia colluding with the colonizing bourgeoisie, which seeks to perpetuate colonial rule through forms of neocolonialism.

Fanon was right to be cautious: he could already see how postcolonial states inhabited by nationalists who came into power after more or less peaceful transitions might be swiftly trapped in dependent relationships to former empires, mired in corruption and ineptitude, and undercut by military coups and insurgencies. Together with his call for constant vigilance against nationalist wrong turns and dead ends, Fanon's vital insight here is that independence cannot in itself ensure the success of a popular struggle for liberation (it is only the beginning) and that true revolution remains the complete transformation of the psyche and liberation from colonialist notions such as race.

The problem with nationalism, of course, was that it had not yet been decolonized, and Fanon is at pains to insist that national consciousness – 'that magnificent song that made the people rise against their oppressors' (*DT* 192, *WE* 163) – must be supplemented in the next revolutionary phase by political and social consciousness. For the national bourgeoisie cultivates a colonialist cultural and raciological politics that it deploys against the emergent national identity forged through anti-colonial violence. Fanon links this back to the precolonial period, which rears its head in the regressive rhetoric of nationalist leaders – one of many 'tragic mishaps' (*DT* 145, *WE* 119) in praxis since it provokes the traumatic memory of intertribal conflict, Muslim–Christian animosity (themes of the cannibal and vandal), and the historical violence between Arab North Africans and sub-Saharan Black Africans, including the African slave trade. As the postcolonial theorist John E. Drabinski points out, Fanon chooses to interpret the Black–Arab conflict 'as merely a restaging of a colonial Manichaeanism rooted in the illusions of ethnicity, race, and missionary religious antagonism'. Fanon also makes no mention of the Caribbean and its place in the Atlantic slave trade, which he appears to repress.[4] The result is what Drabinski calls a double-movement of remembering and forgetting: pursuing the grievances of colonial atrocity while eliding memories of intra-African violence.[5] This explains both the urgency and violence of Fanon's imperative – which fuelled all his recent public interventions – to forget past, precolonial atrocity, and why he holds the messy business of history in such contempt. Misadventure is corrected and put back on course only in the shared commitment to decolonization in the present.

In 'On National Culture', which reproduces his speech at the Second Congress of Black Writers and Artists in Rome in 1959 with some reworkings and a new preface, Fanon repeats his root suspicion of all forms of identity, whether racial or religious, and denigrates those who speak in the name of the unity of African culture (most obviously the practitioners of *négritude* and those associated with *Présence africaine*). At issue is a cultural politics of nationalism as the evolution of a specific, unified and identifiable national culture created by the community of a former colony's native inhabitants, as opposed to a national culture founded on folklore or abstract populism. For Fanon it is the fight for liberation that 'sets culture moving and opens to it the doors of creation' (*DT* 232, *WE* 197), although he says very little here specifically about Algerian culture or the fact that Algerian writers such as Mohammed Dib were exploring ideas of nationalism, preferring instead to focus on sub-Saharan and West Indian culture. His chosen *littérature de combat* is that of Guinea, the only African colony to vote for immediate independence, which it gained in 1958, rather than continued association with France. Fanon cites at length the long prose poem 'Aube africaine' (African Dawn) of 1957 by Keïta Fodéba (also Guinea's minister of the interior), which champions the formation of a revolutionary will out of a history of exploitation and violence. Yet he also misreads the poem, notably its ethnic and symbolic aspects, which relate specifically to the Mandé people rather than to his chosen topic of Guinean national identity (*DT* 215–21, *WE* 183–7). As Christopher L. Miller notes, while he refers to traditional local assemblies and forms of public culture in Africa, Fanon displays little sustained regard for local knowledge, appearing to present precolonial history in ethnocentric terms as no history at all.[6] Again, in sharp contrast to the FLN, which based its future culture on a particular linguistic and ethnic identity, Fanon makes no mention of the Islamic cultural component of an independent Algeria; nor does he address the Arabization of Algeria, made further complicated by the presence of Berber communities and languages. Moreover, he never questions the idea of the nation and national borders, which were artificially established on the African continent by Europeans.

The final chapter, 'Colonial War and Mental Disorders', shifts register abruptly to clinical matters by recording the psychological toll of oppression and resistance on both the colonized and the colonizers. Incorporating earlier written notes on case studies of patients at Blida-Joinville, Fanon offers a comprehensive and harrowing account of the damage wrought by the violence of colonial war. He also refers to his development of ethnopsychiatry while in Tunis treating Algerian combatants and refugees near the border. A series of symptoms and pathologies is presented: from homicidal tendencies in the survivor of a mass slaughter, to the murder by Algerian adolescents of their best friend, the son of settlers, to the torture inflicted by a European inspector on his wife and children. (Subsequent studies have proved Fanon right in his diagnoses regarding servicemen traumatized by their activities as torturers and suffering forms of war neurosis.) The political value of these case studies is clear: to chart the subject's progression from the status of non-engaged civilian to active member of the FLN. The final section ('Criminal Impulses Found in North Africans Which Have Their Origin in the National War of Liberation') is more discursive in form but the aim remains the same: to show that mental illness is an extreme but entirely rational response to an intolerable, 'mad' situation of daily oppression and torture (*DT* 240, *WE* 201). However, one also senses here the residual tensions between Fanon the political militant and Fanon the doctor on the matter of violence, for there is nothing in the clinical case studies about violence as a cleansing force. For Adam Shatz, the chapter's argumentative force throws doubt on the earlier statements made in *Les Damnés* by underlining that, for Fanon, violence was never a simple remedy for the Third World but rather a rite of passage for colonized communities and individuals who had become mentally ill as a result of physical and structural violence and racism.[7] In fact, the chapter reveals that there are two Fanons:

the professional psychiatrist who could admit weakness in his treatment of a patient, and Fanon the political activist always targeting success in populist and messianic tones. As Vergès points out, mental pathology escapes such determinism, and Fanon's voluntaristic political rhetoric is effectively contradicted by his professional practice. It is precisely Fanon's desire to show, as here, that politics and psychology are inseparably linked which ultimately limits his argument that social and cultural emancipation means also psychological emancipation, and thus that alienation is entirely the result of social, cultural and political conditions.[8]

Les Damnés is rounded off by a short conclusion that, while conveying Fanon's lingering ambivalence about the term 'humanism' (that prodigious 'spiritual adventure' which Europe has used to justify colonialism), culminates rousingly with a compensatory Nietzschean expression of will underscored by the repetition of 'Come then, comrades'. Fanon reaffirms the need for violence, not in order to destroy but to liberate and start anew. Europe had the chance to do this but failed: its universalism has proved defunct, and the continent is now suffering, having lost its very sense of humanity. He declares that a 'whole man' will come out of 'total war' and escape the abyss afflicting a Europe mired in 'stasis' and 'obscene narcissism'. Refusing again any knee-jerk, essentializing response, Fanon restates the need for 'true inventions' (*DT* 302, *WE* 252) and 'discoveries' for the sake of all humanity, which must be rehumanized, for 'there is no question of a return to Nature' (*DT* 304, *WE* 232). Yet he deliberately refrains from giving content to this new post-racial humanity, for the 'New Man' belongs still to the future, which marks a definitive break with the past.

Sartre's Boomerang

One of the first readers of *Les Damnés* was Sartre, whose recently published treatise on existential Marxism, *Critique of Dialectical Reason* (1960), exerted a major influence on Fanon. He claimed to have drawn specifically on its analysis of fraternity during his course for ALN soldiers on the Algeria–Tunisia border, and he conceived the unified 'damned of the earth' in manifestly Sartrean terms as a group-in-fusion capable of withdrawing from the seriality of atomized lives in order to form part of a collective project. Sartre was, of course, a committed anti-colonial intellectual, but it was only in September 1960, when he signed the 'Manifeste des 121' – a petition of civil disobedience in protest against the Algerian War and in support of the *insoumis* (that is, those who refused to serve in Algeria) – that he put himself directly on the line for his solidarity with the Algerian cause. For Fanon he was thus the obvious choice to introduce a book that ruled out any mediation with Europe. Fanon first contacted Sartre in the spring of 1961 via Maspero to request a preface, to which Sartre readily agreed. So began their short but eventful collaboration.

In early August, Lanzmann, aided by Maspero, brought Fanon and Sartre together in a hotel outside the centre of Rome, where they were soon joined by Beauvoir, just a matter of days after the new far-right dissident paramilitary group Organisation Armée Secrète (OAS) had set off a bomb outside the Paris apartment Sartre shared with his mother. Fanon spent three days conversing with Sartre, who had now read the complete manuscript. Their first tense and impassioned conversation, with Lanzmann and Beauvoir present, started at lunch and went on into the early hours, exhausting both men. In Beauvoir's fascinating account of the meeting, Fanon reacted testily when she announced that Sartre needed to sleep: 'I don't like people who spare themselves,' he declared to Lanzmann with alpha-male bravado.[9] Fanon talked at length in surprisingly uninhibited fashion about the trials of his life and the liberation struggle, admitting his fears of dying and his natural repulsion for violence and bloodletting of the kind now taking place among Algerian factions. He put his own ambivalence to violence down to being an intellectual, confessing to Sartre that everything he had written about the enfeebled French Left could be applied to himself. Beauvoir noted that when Fanon sought to blame himself for failing to prevent the deaths of Ramdane and Lumumba, he spoke extravagantly, as if he were himself the GPRA ('I'm perhaps paraphrenic,' Fanon ventured by way of justification). Beauvoir could see Fanon was an exceptional man inspired by 'the passion that burned inside him', yet also 'haunted by death' and troubled by a certain remorse for not having been active in his native land – and even more so for not being a native Algerian when, as he insisted, the Algerians were his people.[10] She ascribed his loquacity and bleak sense of humour, which extended to mimicry, to his sense of looming catastrophe, both personal and political (Fanon prophesied that the days following Algeria's independence would be 'terrible').[11] For Beauvoir, who was plainly moved by the pathos of Fanon's fragile state, he appeared condemned, like the damned about whom he was writing.

Sartre duly fulfilled his promise to provide the preface. It was long, wholly sympathetic and, in the words of Maspero, 'beautiful, violent and useful (in any case for us French)' (AF 692). 'The Third World discovers *itself* and speaks to *itself* through this voice' (DT 20, WE 9; original emphasis), Sartre averred, positioning Fanon as a doctor and 'interpreter' of the situation who 'hides nothing' and 'fears nothing' (DT 21, WE 11). Sartre had his own political agenda, of course, writing for a French audience Fanon had ceased to care about (Fanon's principal concern, as he unabashedly told Maspero, was his readership in the Third World, where his book was 'feverishly' awaited (AF 691)). Addressing his fellow Europeans as 'you' and 'we' while effectively putting them on trial, Sartre sought to expose both the 'liberal hypocrisy' of the French (de Gaulle is dismissed as a 'magician') and the operations of the Far Right. He idealized Fanon as a kind of prophet who had seen the light about Europe and was sounding its death knell because 'decolonization has begun' (DT 33, WE 23). This is 'the moment of the boomerang', Sartre announced, when the violence 'comes back on us, it strikes us' (DT 28, WE 17). He implored: 'Let us look at ourselves, if we can bear to, and see what is becoming of us . . . we must face that unexpected revelation, the strip-tease of our humanism . . . it was nothing but an ideology of lies' (DT 31, WE 21).

Yet Fanon's friends and associates viewed Sartre's preface as a distortion and caricature of Fanon's more subtle and considered views as a psychiatrist addressing the violence of colonial racism and the traumas of the colonized. It was not simply that Sartre mangled Fanon as a Manichean thinker when he harnessed the idea of settler Manichaeism to argue that Europeans needed to confront their own complicity ('we in Europe too are being decolonized . . . the settler which is in every one of us is being savagely rooted out'; *DT* 31, *WE* 21). More problematically, Sartre focused almost obsessively on the workings of violence, depicting it with an oracular swagger that Fanon purposely eschewed. For Sartre, rebellion in the Third World was more a wild tribal rampage that had licence to kill all Europeans. 'Read Fanon,' he commanded: 'you will learn how . . . their mad impulse to murder is the expression of the natives' collective unconscious' (*DT* 26, *WE* 16). He followed through exaltedly: 'to shoot down a European is to kill two birds with one stone, to destroy an oppressor and the man he oppresses at the same time; there remain a dead man, and a free man; the survivor, for the first time, feels a *national* soil under his foot' (*DT* 29, *WE* 19; original emphasis).

Fanon knew *Les Damnés* was far from perfect: it was written in a rush against the betrayal of the revolution and that of his own body, and he acknowledged that 'The tone is perhaps sometimes too vehement, but things have come down to the wire.'[12] He may also have become more hardened and uncompromising as he became physically weaker. Yet his theoretical approach to violence remained acutely sensitive and he continued to condemn brutality. He understood the immanence of violence, which marked every relation in the colony and every domain (politics, race, ethics, gender). It is precisely why, for Fanon, violence could not simply be opposed to the human and was inextricable from its very possibility; any new humanism had to avoid the European model based on a separation (itself violent) of humanism from war, genocidal violence and the murderous use of force (*DT* 301, *WE* 251). While he was certainly unequivocal about the necessity of armed violence to achieve genuine decolonization and to avoid remaining in a passive state of self-alienation and bad faith, he also suggested that, in some cases (though not Algeria), the first phase of the liberation of consciousness could actually be accomplished without a violent struggle, for instance through political action and education by an enlightened leadership – this as a first step before the requisite dismantling of the colonial structures by organized forms of violence. Above all, he was fully cognizant of the underlying danger of emancipatory violence, namely that violence does not necessarily lead to the freeing of an individual from their fears and inferiority complexes. If it is accepted that lasting trauma and social maladjustment can be a direct result of participation in violence, the question then becomes: on what conditions does revolutionary violence emancipate, and on what conditions does it alienate? Even if Fanon doesn't explictly pose this question in *Les Damnés*, still less answer it (at this stage in the revolutionary process in Algeria, any final reckoning was impossible), his sober ratiocinations feel more grounded and realistic than Sartre's incendiary preface. When *Les Damnés* appeared in November 1961, the shock of the bloodthirsty preface all but eclipsed the work itself. A watershed in revolutionary thought and writing, the book was immediately denounced by the Right as a frontal assault on Western civilization, while the Left, with the odd exception, automatically censured Fanon for directly addressing the people rather than those in power, and for implying that the European working class were also reaping the rewards of the colonial system.[13]

13

The Final Crossing

Before leaving Rome in August 1961 for Abano Terme, outside Padua, to receive treatment for the spinal injury he had suffered in Morocco two years before, Fanon met secretly with Glissant and Damas, who were encouraged that he was displaying a renewed interest in the Antilles following the riots in Martinique of December 1959. He had written about the events for *El Moudjahid*, in which he stated that they constituted an embryonic revolution – a public stance directly contradicted, however, by the personal view he shared with Sartre and Beauvoir that Martinique was still not ripe for revolution (the riots did, in fact, result in some concessions, with France granting Martinique more rights over legislation at council level).[1] Almost inevitably, Fanon's conversation with Glissant and Damas came to nothing . He met Sartre again very briefly at the end of the month when passing through Rome on his way back to Tunis. He then fell silent. He waited in vain for Benyoucef Benkhedda, newly nominated as president of the GPRA, to summon him to Belgrade to attend the conference of heads of state of non-aligned countries that was to begin in early September. Fanon's health was now worsening dramatically, and he suffered a major relapse. He was extremely frail, unable even to talk. In October his condition became so serious that he eventually overcame his deep-rooted reluctance to receive medical care in the United States, meeting Sartre one last time in Rome en route from Tunis to New York, then travelling down to Washington, DC. When he arrived in the American capital on 3 October under the *nom de guerre* Ibrahim Fanon, he spent the first week alone at the Dupont Circle Hotel. He was then taken on 10 October to the National Institutes of Health Clinical Center at Bethesda, just outside the capital, to be treated by Dr David Haywood. He was dying.

A brief period of relative recovery followed, with highs and lows linked to the various treatments to which Fanon was subjected. Josie, who was made a guest of the Guinean embassy along with the now six-year-old Olivier, was continually by his side and in touch by phone with Beauvoir. He received visits from African representatives to the UN as well as Holden Roberto. In November, Fanon dictated to Josie a letter for his friend and confidant in Tunis Roger Taïeb, a pharmacist and executive member of the Tunisian Communist Party, in which he explained his condition: 'If I had left Tunis four days later, well, I would have been dead . . . I am in the difficult period following great hemorrhages during which the leukemic process still multiplies its offensive, during which I am supervised day and night, given injections of the elements of blood that I am terribly missing and large transfusions to stay in shape, which is to say, alive.'[2] For Lanzmann, Fanon was living his death minute by minute and resisting it 'savagely',[3] confident that he could beat the disease through willpower alone while also harbouring plans for future books – one called 'The Leukaemic and His Double', the other a history of the ALN. At the end of the month he received a copy of *Les Damnés* from Maspero. Sartre's preface was read out to him (his opinion is unknown), along with letters from friends who had read the book. Yet Fanon could feel catastrophe approaching and he was suspicious of all hospital staff. In one reported anecdote he experienced the terrifying recurring fantasy of being 'lactified' by a new denegrification serum. As on the battlefield in the Second World War, he wished to anticipate the hour of his death – a dignified death of his own choosing. The cruel irony, however, was that he was dying from an abnormal build-up of *white* cells in the bone marrow that prevented the body from producing healthy red blood cells, leading to an increase in the blood of white globules. Lanzmann was in touch with a French doctor who had found a new way to fight leukaemia by renewing the entire blood system; he was even on his way to Washington but arrived too late. On 3 December,

Fanon was struck with an attack of double bronchopneumonia. At two o'clock in the morning on 6 December 1961, Frantz Omar Ibrahim Fanon died.

On the day news of Fanon's death reached Paris, copies of *Les Damnés* were being seized in French bookstores on grounds of sedition and being a threat to national security. His image was suddenly everywhere, inspiring Beauvoir to write that 'His death weighed heavily because he had charged his death with all the intensity of his life.'[4] Yet Fanon's final journey had still to take place: the return of his body first to Tunis, then across the border to Algeria, in accordance with his reported last wishes before departing for the United States that his body be brought back to Africa and buried on Algerian soil. On 11 December a specially commissioned plane transported Fanon's coffin to Tunis, where it was displayed at the headquarters of the GPRA. The next day, after a commemorative speech by Krim Belkacem, vice-president of the GPRA and minister of the interior ('Frantz Fanon! You devoted your life to the cause of freedom, dignity, justice, and the good,' he proclaimed), the coffin was taken to the town of Ghardimaou near the Tunisian border and delivered to the ALN. Carrying the coffin on a stretcher, a dozen ALN soldiers then carefully crossed the border (the fence carried a 30,000-watt electric charge) into recently liberated Algerian territory, accompanied by close friends of Fanon including Taïeb and Chaulet and joined along the way by local people who hailed 'El Hakim' (the doctor). After the ALN commander Ali Mendejli had eloquently saluted 'Omar Ibrahim-Frantz Fanon' as a 'sincere militant' in Arabic, his body, along with copies of *Peau noire*, *L'An v* and *Les Damnés*, was buried in the Cemetery of the Martyrs (Chouhadas) of Sifana in a wooded area near Hammam Sidi Trad, a mere 600 metres (2,000 ft) inside the border. The FLN and ALN were burying Fanon heroically as one of their own, as he would have wished.[5] Yet his tragically premature death denied him the satisfaction of witnessing Algeria finally gain its independence three months later with the signing of the Évian Accords. The former head of the ALN, Houari Boumédienne, and his Armée Nationale Populaire arrived triumphantly in Algiers on 9 September 1962.

Fanon's body transported by FLN soldiers across the border from Tunisia to Algerian soil, 12 December 1961.

A number of mysteries surrounding Fanon's death and final crossing remain, starting with the very cause of his illness. This perplexed Fanon himself, since no other sibling had ever displayed symptoms of acute myeloid leukaemia. He suspected it could have originated in the accident in Morocco: FLN operatives were targeted by the French 11th Paratrooper Battalion, whose members had a radioactive substance sewn into the lining of certain suits. This is still a defence secret, however, and cannot be proved.[6] Or perhaps there was a link between his condition and the malaria Josie suffered in Accra that would affect her for the rest of her life? A definitive connection between malaria infection and cancer progression, beyond the coinfection of malaria, has yet to be established. However, those chronically infected with certain pathogens are at increased risk of developing lymphomas. One sub-group for example, Burkitt lymphoma, a common form of childhood cancer, is frequent in areas of equatorial Africa endemic for malaria.

Other mysteries relate to Fanon's passage to the USA, which was kept secret from most in his entourage. The official line is that the GPRA (specifically the former FLN minister of information in Tunis,

M'Hamed Yazid, and the GPRA's representative in Rome, Taïeb Boulahrouf) was in contact with American diplomacy and took care of all practicalities. But the circumstances of Fanon's arrival in Washington appeared dubious. A bureaucratic problem over papers (or, according to other sources, a preliminary medical exam) meant that Fanon received no care for a week before being taken to the hospital where there were plenty of beds. Beauvoir claimed he had been deliberately abandoned but does not directly accuse the CIA of involvement.[7] However, the widespread belief that Fanon 'died in the arms of the CIA' has never been entirely cleared up. On 21 February 1969 the *Washington Post* published a piece by the conservative journalist Joseph Alsop, who alleged that the CIA were responsible for Fanon's transportation from Tunis and that Ollie Iselin, a member of the American diplomatic corps in North Africa, had been appointed by the CIA as Fanon's case officer to escort him from Tunisia to the United States.[8] It is certainly a fact that Iselin arranged for Fanon, Josie and Olivier to fly to Washington and personally visited Fanon in hospital on a daily basis (Alsop referred in his article to 'downright brotherly visits'). Iselin also attended the burial in Algeria, a fact confirmed by photographs published in *El Moudjahid*. Alsop was clearly attempting to sow doubts in the minds of Fanon's mounting leftist admirers by implying he was compromised by contact with the CIA, although it seems Fanon did not suspect Iselin was a CIA official.[9] While never himself a member of the GPRA, Fanon was close to people who were, so could potentially have provided useful information. Although she was not with him to the end, having already returned to Tunis (something she later claimed to regret, for 'he died alone'[10]), Josie adamantly denied the rumour that the CIA managed to obtain secrets from her dying husband, who was, of course, uniquely equipped to withstand interrogation techniques. Yazid similarly downplayed Alsop's revelation, stating that Fanon was attended by many people, including the FLN's New York delegation and Black American activists. A recent attempt by the American scholar Simone Browne to retrieve under the Freedom of Information Act documents held by the CIA and FBI pertaining to Fanon did not produce anything new.[11]

Another source of confusion concerns the location of Fanon's body. The unofficial burial was a propaganda coup on the part of the GPRA to show the French that they could pull off such a daring manoeuvre on Algerian territory. And it worked: three days after the ceremony, a number of French officers responsible for the sector were relieved of their duties because they had allowed it to take place. Once this had been achieved, however, the Algerian authorities appeared to care little about the actual grave. In 1964, acting on behalf of his mother, Joby attempted to establish from the Algerian authorities where exactly his brother was buried in the hope of taking his remains back to Martinique. He also wanted to see the document in which Fanon expressed his wish to be interred in Algerian territory. He met Boumédienne in person, but to no avail. When he then applied for the certificate of Fanon's death, he discovered it was mysteriously lost, along with a black plastic envelope containing personal documents (including his brother's final wishes) that should have been kept with the body as it was transported across national borders.[12] Joby hit a brick wall. To rub further salt into the wound, both Boumédienne and Louanchi of the FLN declared that Fanon's name could not be added to the colossal monument to the glory of the revolution martyrs being planned for Algiers because the site of his burial during the war was unknown.

Were these administrative evasions simply a mark of the Algerian state's commitment to ensuring that the body of a martyr remained untouched on Algerian soil? Or did they indicate a desire to remove Fanon from public memory in Algeria as the country became increasingly authoritarian and distant from Fanon's vision of 'an Algeria open to all, in which every kind of genius can grow' (AV 14, ADC 33)? Certainly, Fanon's warning of neocolonial continuity between the colony and the postcolony was becoming embarrassing to the new order, and his ideas were progressively being dismissed as alien – the speculations of a Black Antillean who had a White French wife and couldn't speak Arabic. However, immediately following Boumédienne's bloodless coup and ousting of Ahmed Ben Bella in the summer of 1965, Fanon's remains were formally transferred and laid to rest at the Cemetery of the Martyrs in the village of Aïn El Kerma, in the *wilaya* of El Tarf. The tombstone bore the inscription (in Arab) 'Doctor Ibrahim Frantz Fanon' and was dated 20 July 1965. Joby subsequently found out in 1982 when visiting Aïn El Kerma that Fanon's body had, in fact, been exhumed, moved and reinterred soon after the initial burial, although no one in the top Algerian ranks wished to acknowledge it. The truth was revealed by a former Algerian combatant whom Fanon had once treated and personally nursed for a major wound: he claimed to have discovered and extracted the coffin from the provisional grave, which at that point still contained the envelope of documents.[13] It was ultimately left to a tribunal in Fort-de-France in March 1982 to declare that the Ibrahim Fanon of Tunisian nationality who died on 6 December 1961 was indeed Frantz Fanon.

This leaves a final mystery in the Fanon story. Up until her death in 1989 Josie actively guarded and shaped her husband's legacy. She approved the material collected in *Pour la révolution africaine* and insisted that Sartre's preface to *Les Damnés* be removed from the book when it was republished by Maspero in 1968 owing to Sartre's pro-Zionist views and active support of Israel during the Six-Day War of June 1967. (It was not until 1985 that the preface was fully restored

Fanon's final resting place at Aïn El Kerma, Algeria.

to French editions.) In addition to her work for the Algerian press (for example, interviewing Che Guevara when he visited Algiers in July 1963), she contributed to the news magazine *Jeune Afrique* (originally published in Tunis) and, from 1977, to the French Pan-African monthly *Demain l'Afrique*. She never wrote a memoir, however, and the rare personal interviews she gave in which she talked about her career (for example, to Radio Haïti in 1979[14]) were always framed as 'professional'. If she did touch on the life and work of Fanon, she scrupulously avoided personal issues. In October 1988 Josie watched from the balcony of her flat in the suburb of El Biar in Algiers as young people protesting against high unemployment, rising prices and autocratic rule began burning police cars in the streets. The riots spread to other cities, and the police responded with the kind of extreme violence that had marked French colonialism, resulting in more than five hundred dead and a thousand injured within a week. Nine months later, on 13 July 1989, Josie jumped from her fifth-floor window to her death.

The official line is that it was suicide. According to her close friend Assia Djebar, Josie had recently visited Fanon's grave and the places in Tunis where they had lived before returning to Algiers to put her affairs in order (letters from Frantz, photographs and so forth).[15] She spent a week in hospital owing to mental fatigue and depression,[16] and, two days before her death, was possibly also the victim of a street assault in central Algiers.[17] In fact, Josie had not been in a good way for a while, disclosing in a letter to Lanzmann that she had tried to take her own life a few years before.[18] However, granted that the manner of her passing has been a classic CIA method of assassination and that Fanon's final days were overseen by the CIA, other causes cannot be entirely ruled out, either involving the CIA or made to look as if so. What was so important about Josie that ultimately needed to be silenced? The question will doubtless remain unresolved. Josie was buried in the Muslim El Kettar cemetery in Algiers as 'Nadia', the Arab name she used when living semi-clandestinely with Fanon. Subsequent attempts by Olivier, an Algerian national by choice, to have his parents reinterred together have failed. For Algerians, Fanon alone is their martyr.

14

Fanon's After-Lives

'Each generation must, out of relative obscurity, discover its mission,
fulfil it, or betray it.'
(*DT* 197, *WE* 166)

In his death-bed letter to Roger Taïeb, in which he emphasized his
long familiarity with the prospect of death, Fanon touched on his
potential future legacy: 'what matters is not to know whether we
can escape it [death] but whether we have achieved the maximum
for the ideas we have made our own . . . We are nothing on earth
if we are not first of all slaves to a cause, the cause of the people,
the cause of justice and liberty.' He added, with a characteristically
dramatic touch: 'I want you to know that even at the moment
when the doctors had despaired I still thought (oh, in what a fog!),
I thought of the Algerian people, of the people of the Third World
and if I survived it is because of them.'[1] Legend dictates accordingly
that, following his death, Fanon became a poster boy both for
Third Worldism (which he helped create, in the belief that new
African states would instigate a new humanism and socialism)
and for revolution, spurring national liberation movements and
other radical political organizations across the globe, including in
Palestine, Sri Lanka, apartheid-era South Africa and the USA. The
new People's Democratic Republic of Algeria was briefly the leading
light of the Non-Aligned Movement, and Algiers became a hub of
anti-imperialism, anti-racism and world revolution, welcoming the
ANC, the PLO, the Black Panther Party and other national liberation
movements. Many of these were deeply influenced by Fanon's

utopian, visionary works, which were now becoming available in translation, inspiring figures from Steve Biko to Stokely Carmichael, who also hailed Fanon (wrongly) as a Black nationalist. The Black Panthers' work on prisoner reintegration and public health initiatives was directly galvanized by Fanon's work on the medicalization of criminality featured in *Les Damnés*. Hannah Arendt's disapproval in 1970 of Fanon's vision of a comradeship under arms driving social revolution (the taste of power provided by violent revolt is fleeting, she asserted, holding Fanon mainly to blame for the 'glorification of violence' by the student movements of the late 1960s) only added to his radical allure.[2]

The process of Fanon's legacy and his generative translatability were not made easy by the fact that he is one of the few major thinkers whose work has been translated by different translators, and not always accurately. Moreover, as the postcolonial theorist Andrew M. Daily states, Fanon 'never outlined a positive political vision that would command political fealty outside his unstinting opposition to those forces that annihilated humanity, colonialism above all else'.[3] Further, as Matthieu Renault suggests, while Fanon's writings herald the beginnings of a certain wartime postcolonialism at the heart of anti-colonialism, they also predict the difficulties of current postcolonial theory to theorize violence and consider war together with the decolonization of knowledge.[4] These various factors, along with some of the contradictions and intractable mysteries of Fanon traced in this volume, have led commentators and theorists to dice and splice his work in order to respin it – from the Marxist Fanon to the revolutionary Fanon to the postcolonial Fanon – in a bid to define and fix 'Fanonism'. Recognizing two radically different Fanons – a dominant Fanon who conceives of change as a dialectical process of becoming, and a 'subterranean Fanon' who experiments with an even more explosive underground theory of 'transformation' that entails the complete destruction of colonial structures of oppression – Gavin Arnall proposes quite sensibly that we do not need to choose between the two in a futile attempt to reconcile them.[5]

Still, how does one best remember someone who insisted that he belonged 'irreducibly' to his time (*PN* 10, *BS* 15) while his work courses so ardently with futurity? In his foreword to the 1986 English edition of *Peau noire*, Homi Bhabha contends that 'Remembering is never a quiet act of introspection or retrospection. It is a painful re-membering, a putting together of the dismembered past to make sense of the trauma of the present. It is such a memory of the history of race and racism, colonialism and the question of cultural identity, that Fanon reveals with greater profundity and poetry than any other writer' (*BS* xxiii–xxiv). In Fanon's case, it is an ineluctable fact that historical accounts of the Algerian Revolution, in line with modern Arab Islamic nationalism, do not accord him a major role, and he has never been fully integrated into the pantheon of Algerian nationalism (the posthumous award of the Prix National des Lettres Algériennes in 1963 is a rare exception). The odd street, hospital and *lycée* in Algeria is named after him, and Blida-Joinville is now the Hôpital Psychiatrique Frantz-Fanon de Blida, where a museum in his honour is due to open in 2023, but otherwise his influence there seems relatively invisible. Indeed, had he lived to see a free Algeria, Fanon, as a Black agnostic from the French Antilles who fought for a pluri-ethnic, pluri-religious and pluri-linguistic nation, may have found himself no more than an honorary Algerian – perhaps even an exile – in his chosen homeland. In line with the FLN's original demand, the new Code of Nationality defined nationality in both ethnic and religious terms, making Islam the state religion. This meant, for example, that the brave women of the *maquis* witnessed a severe curtailment of their rights after independence. In Algeria, the past can never simply just disappear, and together Algerian culture and Islam have arguably taken their revenge on the present, including even the revolution itself.

Despite the various efforts of Fanon's family – not only Josie, Joby (who died in 2004) and Olivier but his 'lost' daughter Mireille Fanon Mendès-France, president of the Fondation Frantz-Fanon, founded in 2007[6] – to keep his flame alive, Fanon's legacy in the other major regions he traversed has been likewise chequered, though for different reasons. In Martinique, for instance, where he is considered a revolutionary who pursued his revolution far from the Antilles, Fanon remains largely forgotten. Those who continue to view him as a traitor both to Martinique and to France have even sought to banish his memory.[7] There is no Fanonist party (*Peau noire* was not, after all, a pro-independence manifesto), and the 1982 Memorial International conference in Fort-de-France honouring Fanon, organized with the help of Manville, was not supported by a political party. Yet Fanon helped shape French Caribbean students, activists and intellectuals through his blazingly honest critique of the Antillean psyche, assimilation, nationalism and *négritude* – poets and writers such as Daniel Boukman, Maryse Condé, Sonny Rupaire, Bertène Juminer, Raphaël Confiant and Patrick Chamoiseau; critics and social scientists including Glissant, Roland Suvélor and Michel Giraud; and many others.[8] For Glissant, Fanon's decision to break from Martinique and become Algerian was the 'only true event in Antillean history', even though in the process Fanon fatally ignored the memory of the 'Martinican problem' (that is, the slave trade).[9] Glissant argued that only when Antilleans have recognized their historical becoming as a people and overcome their 'unconscious refusal of structures' will they be able to 'tear' themselves from their trauma and launch the 'initial and initiating act' of a 'politics and poetics of liberation', which would finally 'enroot' them in their proper world.[10] The writers linked to his journal *ACOMA* (1971–3) sought to go beyond Fanon's initial prescriptions: where Fanon called for a restored humanism and a new world, they promoted *enracinement* in the Caribbean and the 'Other America'.

In France, where he officially remained a deserter, Fanon was essentially dismissed as obsolete in the period up to 2000 during which the conflict in Algeria was still referred to by some as a 'peace-keeping operation'. *L'An v* even fell out of print after 1982. French academics have since mobilized Fanon specifically to support or oppose the adoption of postcolonial studies. Casting Fanon as a precocious critic of the postcolonial state and an alternative to Anglo-Indian postcolonial studies, Jean-François Bayart, for instance, has distinguished Fanon's activist work against colonialism from the 'theoreticians of Postcolonial Studies, more preoccupied with their university careers than concrete engagement at the side of the subalterns'.[11] However, a new generation of intellectuals and militants in France has embraced Fanon, in particular the Algerian Fanon, who was always kept separate from the Antillean Fanon. Norman Ajari, for example, completed in 2014 a pioneering doctoral thesis at Toulouse University showing how Fanon developed a 'speculative politics' in response to colonial dehumanization. The trailblazing film director Claire Denis repeatedly insists in her work on Fanon's continuing relevance for understanding the ambient discourse of racism and the violence of racialized thinking. Meanwhile, on the 60th anniversary of his death, in April 2021, Fanon's life and work were celebrated on French public radio with a major four-part series entitled 'Révolution Fanon'.[12] However, there is still no psychiatric institution in France bearing Fanon's name. More generally, although President Emmanuel Macron's declassification in 2021 of secret French military files and documents relating to the French–Algerian War led to an official report by the historian Benjamin Stora on the 'memories of colonization and the Algerian War' (part of France's belated response to the painful legacy of decolonization), no apology or offer of reparation or restitution, as Fanon once called for, has been issued.

The ambivalent reception to Fanon in Algeria, Martinique and France contrasts dramatically with the way his work has been taken up in the Anglo-American world. His extraordinary fluidity and reach, together with his commitment to moving beyond the dictates of historicity and identity, have ensured the continually growing impact of his work, making him what Henry Louis Gates Jr has called a new type of 'global theorist'.[13] In social theory and cultural studies, where Fanonian concepts inform discussions of race, nation, migration, language, representation and visuality, his influence has been a catalyst for radical thought and the creation of new genealogies. To take just two recent examples: Anthony Alessandrini's *Frantz Fanon and the Future of Cultural Politics: Finding Something Different* (2014) brings Fanon freely into conversation with a range of figures including Said, Foucault and Jamaica Kincaid to think through the popular uprisings of the Arab Spring in the early 2010s;[14] and Nigel C. Gibson's 2021 collection *Fanon Today: Reason and Revolt*

A mural painting of Fanon by Bruce Clarke in Vénissieux, Lyon, 2015.

of the Wretched of the Earth presents new transglobal approaches to Fanonian praxis, focusing on activist movements of resistance and mass revolutionary uprisings in response to repression or state violence, including practices around COVID-19 in the Global South.[15] In his introduction to the 60th anniversary Grove Press edition of *The Wretched of the Earth*, in which he salutes Fanon as the revolutionary intellectual 'most relevant for the twenty-first century' on account of his 'intense Socratic energy' aligned with 'African self-criticism', the African American philosopher and theorist Cornel West concludes resoundingly: 'For Fanon, revolutionary internationalism – anti-imperialist, anti-capitalist, anti-colonialist, anti-patriarchal, and anti-white-supremacist – yields a new humanism that puts a premium on the psychic, social, and political needs of poor and working peoples – a solidarity and universality from below.'[16]

Scholars such as West are responding to Fanon's comprehensive project both to decolonize and deracialize society and culture by moving beyond notions of racial identity. However, Fanon's importance in current global debates – his revolutionary breath – is ironically most visible in the new generation of Black identity politics. During the protests in the United States that began in 2020 against the killing of unarmed Black people by police, members of the Black Lives Matter social movement attributed to Fanon words about deathly suffocation that went viral: 'When we revolt, it's not for a particular culture. We revolt simply because, for many reasons, we can no longer breathe' (an approximation of a sentence from the final page of *Peau noire*: 'It was, in more than one way, becoming impossible for him [the Indo-Chinese man] to breathe'; *PN* 183, *BS* 226). Black Lives Matter extends in part the movement of Afro-pessimism that draws directly on Fanon's understanding of racial exclusion and marginalization to pursue the links between Blackness, negativity and violence in Western society, arguing that the existence of Blackness has been foundationally built upon anti-Black violence, and that the condition of Blackness is unique: at once coterminous with slaveness and synonymous with social death. Propelled by Fanon's anti-essentializing philosophy of anti-difference, whereby the Black does not exist any more than the White, Frank B. Wilderson III theorizes Blackness as a condition of – or relation to – ontological death, as opposed to a cultural identity or human subjectivity.[17] Blackness is thus created through the denial of self-definition rather than through any experience or quality preceding that denial or existing beyond it. Wilderson's version of Afro-pessimism proposes liberation within consciousness as a 'work of understanding', as opposed to most contemporary discourse, which posits utopian, solution-based frameworks.[18]

Afro-pessimism has been interpreted and developed by other Black theorists who turn to the same areas where the sutures of anti-Blackness appear to be drawn the tightest, and yet who find reasons for some optimism. In *In the Wake: On Blackness and Being* (2016), Christina Sharpe looks to the hold of the slave ship to recover a sense of relationality, turning 'hold' itself into community responsibility and witnessing.[19] Nahum Dimitri Chandler uses jazz poetics in his 2013 book, *X – The Problem of the Negro as a Problem for Thought*, to insist on variability within Black subjectivity without denying its existence as a discrete and specific mode of being.[20] Meanwhile, Paul Gilroy employs Fanon to take direct issue with the radical negativity of Afro-pessimism, proposing instead a positive humanism based on post-race universalism. Gilroy sees Afro-pessimism as part of an ontological turn 'in which race becomes an unassailable barrier between the self and the world, and anti-Black violence an immutable fact'.[21] Invoking Fanon's conclusion to *Peau noire* about overcoming history as the very point from which 'the history of blackness appeals to the future', Gilroy argues that Fanon offers a propitious political starting point for today, 'first by resistance to white supremacy and then by the uncomfortable acceptance that we are no longer what we once were and cannot rewind the tapes of our complex cultural life to a single knowable point of origin'.[22] Gilroy calls persuasively for a new kind of postcolonial cosmopolitanism based on planetary inquiry and leading to new forms of kinship and worldly conversation about sociality and humanity.[23]

Such crucial debates in current Black critical studies testify to the vitalizing complexities of Fanon's thought and suggest that, rather than aim for a final and definitive verdict on his multi-corpus, we need to continue to read through, with, yet also *against* it. A key instance of this challenge in action can be found in the work of the Cameroonian philosopher and political theorist Achille Mbembe, who has been highly critical of Fanon's commitment to absolute violence and what he calls 'the Fanonian cul-de-sac', that is, 'the dead-end of the generalized circulation and exchange of death as the condition for being human'.[24] Mbembe questions Fanon's argument for violence in *Les Damnés* as a duty and politico-ethical responsibility, since taking the life of a heavily armed enemy also risks in the same moment taking one's own life (that is, self-sacrifice), provoking the question how the logic of murder is ultimately different from that of suicide. Yet Mbembe has also sought, with reference to the concept of 'viscerality', to restore the underlying unity in Fanon between the political and the clinical/psychiatric, which have often been kept apart but which form a common dialectic in his work.[25] In the chapter 'Fanon's Pharmacy' in *Necropolitics* (2019), Mbembe tracks the lethal afterlife of sovereign power as it subjects whole populations to what Fanon called 'the zone of nonbeing'. Alert to Fanon's dual interest in histories of violence (destruction) and the therapeutic process (life), Mbembe draws on Fanon's notion of the 'relation of care' as a shared vulnerability in the clinical care relation, whereby the patient is reborn again in the world and seeks to become once more the origin of the future. Medicine, Mbembe argues, reveals that humanity-in-creation is a product of the encounter with the 'face of the other', this person who reveals me to myself. It begins with a gesture related to speech – that is, that which makes a relationship (the relation of care) possible. Such conceptions allow one to encounter the Other not as a thing to exclude, but rather as a person with whom to build a more just world.[26] Mbembe ends his study with Fanon's figure of the *passant* to propose a new ethics of the 'passerby' as emblematic of the 'elsewhere' that relies less on sovereign power than on transnational resistance to the global spread of necropolitics.[27] Fanon, he boldly concludes, is the author of a powerful new humanism *beyond* the human – a humanism that he clung to desperately and which is at once compensatory and noble.

Another area of major difficulty in Fanon's work has, of course, been his hypermasculinism and flawed understanding of sexuality and sexual politics, in particular his proscriptive attitude to homosexuality in *Peau noire.* It was a blind spot that persisted to the end, as when in conversation with Sartre and Beauvoir in Rome he used the case of a (White) upper-class gay man living in the colonies to condemn homosexuality as a form of psychosis, social disintegration and mental decomposition.[28] Yet such contentious views have also stimulated postcolonial feminist and queer critics to interrogate Fanon's analysis of gender and sexuality in the context of his dialectics of liberation, including his ethos of love and solidarity expressed in statements of human receptivity such as: 'As soon as I *desire* I am asking to be considered. I am not merely here-and-now, sealed into thingness . . . I do battle for the creation of a human world – that is, of a world of reciprocal recognitions' (*PN* 177, *BS* 218; original emphasis). As the African Studies scholar Ayo A. Coly has written: 'Reading Fanon today, against the backdrop of queer theory, his injunction to violence, his programme of "complete disorder" and "creation of a new man", are a call for a queering of the self, an unthinking of received categories and scripts of identities.'[29] The postcolonial critic C. L. Quinan claims similarly that, 'with its investment in non-normative futurities and its focus on unbecoming, Fanon's brand of decolonization was, in many senses, queer'.[30] Furthermore, many intergenerational Black queer visual artists have not only addressed his ideas but transgressed them in order to rethink the nature of Black homosexuality, masculinity and femininity – artists such as the late Nigerian-born photographer Rotimi Fani-Kayodé and Ghanaian artist Eric Gyamfi, who have responded directly to Fanon's premise that Black subjects need to self-reflect and self-analyse.[31] The groundbreaking 1996 film *Frantz Fanon: Black Skin White Mask* by gay British filmmakers Isaac Julien and Mark Nash, which spearheaded new critical approaches to Fanon in Anglo-Saxon postcolonial theory and philosophy, was an experimental docudrama combining archive footage, interviews with Fanon's family and friends and postcolonial scholars like Hall and Vergès, and poetic reconstructions of Fanon's life. The film dares to suggest that Fanon's theories might be used to think constructively about Black homosexuality, as when, upon mention on the soundtrack that Fanon suddenly glimpses a Black man during a moment of hallucination, the authorial figure of Julien himself slips briefly into view to assert a queer filiation.[32]

These powerful and inventive forms of critical engagement with the multiple cross-currents of Fanon's oeuvre reveal it to be both a dynamic springboard and a vital touchstone for addressing fundamental questions about the contemporary condition, despite – yet also precisely because of – its theoretical knots and disparities. They underline that Fanon's legacy cannot easily be co-opted, and that no one nation or generation can lay unique claim to him: he remains an unclassifiable and transhistorical free agent of individual thinking and self-transformation, unbound by the demands and expectations of truth, identity and rational knowledge. As Cherki eloquently put it in her 2011 reflection on Fanon's legacy fifty years on – in which she also acknowledged the paradox of Fanon at once promoting universality while insisting on the subject's history from one generation to another – his practice of critique 'encourages the opening up of a (third) zone in which a historicity, whose legacy we carry, might be articulated, a zone in which we might gain awareness of our own alienation'.[33] The enduring example of Fanon – fearless in the cause of social justice, defiant in his refusal of all orthodoxies, unstinting in his attention to the body's cry – summons us to take a similar creative leap of faith into the unfamiliar as a potential first step on the long road to achieving genuine change.

References

Introduction: Fanon: Doctor, Writer, Revolutionary

1 See Daniel Boukman, *Frantz Fanon: Traces d'une vie exemplaire* (Paris, 2016).
2 See Joby Fanon, *Frantz Fanon: De la Martinique à l'Algérie et à l'Afrique* (Paris, 2004), pp. 181–2, where he takes particular aim at the 'fantasies' promoted by Alice Cherki in her biography of Fanon, *Frantz Fanon, portrait* (Paris, 2000).
3 Stuart Hall, 'Why Fanon?' [1996], in Hall, *Selected Writings on Race and Difference*, ed. Paul Gilroy and Ruth Wilson Gilmore, ebook (Durham, NC, 2021), pp. 339–57 (339).
4 Albert Memmi, 'The Impossible Life of Frantz Fanon', *Massachusetts Review*, XIV/1 (1973), pp. 9–39 (17).
5 J. Fanon, *Frantz Fanon*, p. 135.
6 The volume *Frantz Fanon: Alienation and Freedom*, ed. Jean Khalfa and Robert J. C. Young, trans. Steven Corcoran (London and New York, 2018), brings together for the first time in English previously unavailable and unpublished material, including Fanon's psychiatry thesis, scientific articles written during the 1950s, the two extant plays written in Lyon, scientific articles and editorials for internal hospital newspapers, letters, and a catalogue of Fanon's library along with annotations to his books.

1 More French than French: Boyhood on a Colonial Island

1 In descending order of age: Mireille (also Fanon's godmother), Félix, Gabrielle, Joby, Frantz, Marie-Flore, Marie-Rose and Willy.
2 In an interview with David Macey, cited in David Macey, *Frantz Fanon: A Biography*, ebook (London, 2012), p. 44.

3 Marcel Manville, *Les Antilles sans fard* (Paris, 1992), p. 245.
4 Fanon later wrote in one letter to his mother, in November 1947, that he forbade himself from being sentimental.
5 Alice Cherki, *Frantz Fanon, portrait* (Paris, 2000), p. 18.
6 David Macey, *Frantz Fanon: A Biography*, ebook (London, 2012), p. 61.
7 Rita Maran, *Torture: The Role of Ideology in the French–Algerian War* (New York, 1989), p. 5.
8 See *PN* 34–42, *BS* 42–52.

2 Fighting for the Republic: From *Dissidence* to Combat

1 See *PRA* 28–30, *TAR* 19–20.
2 Joby Fanon, *Frantz Fanon: De la Martinique à l'Algérie et à l'Afrique* (Paris, 2004), p. 56.
3 Ibid., p. 59.
4 Ibid., p. 237.
5 I borrow this important opposition from David Macey, *Frantz Fanon: A Biography*, ebook (London, 2012), p. 98.
6 See Charles de Gaulle, *Mémoires de Guerre*, vol. III (Paris, 1959), p. 33. I am grateful to Charles Evans and Brice Montaner for providing this reference in 'Blanchiment in the French Army?', https://ww2experiences.blogspot.com, 18 September 2012.
7 J. Fanon, *Frantz Fanon*, p. 239.
8 Ibid., p. 64.
9 In a letter from Fanon to his *marraine de guerre*, cited ibid., p. 111. No further details of this episode are supplied by Fanon.
10 Ibid., pp. 69–70.
11 See ibid., pp. 69–70 (69).
12 Ibid.
13 Ibid., p. 70.
14 Ibid., pp. 69–70.
15 Alice Cherki, *Frantz Fanon, portrait* (Paris, 2000), p. 25.
16 This is the view of his brother Joby, expressed in J. Fanon, *Frantz Fanon*, p. 135.
17 Cited in David Macey, *Frantz Fanon: A Biography*, ebook (London, 2012), p. 106.

3 Return to the Native Land: With and Against Césaire

1 See *PN* 72, *BS* 90.
2 *Tropiques: Collection complète, 1941–1945* (Paris, 1978), p. 39.
3 Jane Hiddleston, *Understanding Postcolonialism* (Stocksfield, 2009), pp. 33–4.
4 Ibid., pp. 34–5.
5 Ibid., p. 33.
6 See Fred Moten, 'Blackness and Nothingness (Mysticism in the Flesh)', *South Atlantic Quarterly*, CXII/4 (2013), pp. 738–80.
7 Aimé Césaire in 'Hommages à Frantz Fanon', *Présence africaine*, XL (1962), pp. 119–22 (119). See also Césaire's obituary of Fanon in *Jeune Afrique*, 13–19 December 1961.
8 Aimé Césaire, 'Par tous mots guerrier-silex', in *Moi, luminaire . . .* (Paris, 1982), pp. 20–21.
9 Césaire in 'Hommages à Frantz Fanon', p. 120.
10 Ibid.

4 The Voyage In: Love and Loathing in Lyon

1 Marcel Manville, *Les Antilles sans fard* (Paris, 1992), p. 242.
2 See Edward Said, *Culture and Imperialism* [1993] (New York, 1998), pp. 242–3.
3 Joby Fanon, *Frantz Fanon: De la Martinique à l'Algérie et à l'Afrique* (Paris, 2004), p. 111.
4 Ibid.
5 Ibid.
6 On Joby's initiative, Mireille later became part of the extended Fanon family.
7 J. Fanon, *Frantz Fanon*, pp. 135–6.
8 Ibid., p. 141. This statement by Joby introduces a passage by Fanon (context not provided) in which he talks about 'the words of the tramp' and refers to 'bow-words', 'bullet-words', 'saw-words' and 'words conducting ions'.
9 From a letter written by Maspero in September 1963, cited in *AF*, p. 29.
10 J. Fanon, *Frantz Fanon*, p. 130.
11 Fanon writes of this experiment in *Peau noire*, where he explains that when the word *nègre* was introduced, it triggered for over half the respondents 'biology, penis, strong, athletic, potent, boxer,

Joe Louis, Jesse Owens, Senegalese troops, savage, animal, devil, sin' (*PN* 134, *BS* 166). (In the original French Fanon refers to 'Jess Owen'.)

12　The full title is 'Mental alterations, character modifications, psychic disorders and intellectual deficit in spinocerebellar heredodegeneration: A case of Friedreich's ataxia with delusions of possession'.

13　See Jean Khalfa's excellent overview of Fanon's career in psychiatry: 'Fanon and Psychiatry', *Nottingham French Studies*, LIV/1 (2015), pp. 52–71.

14　J. Fanon, *Frantz Fanon*, p. 149. Fanon suggests the quotation is from Nietzsche's *Thus Spoke Zarathustra*, but, as Khalfa explains in *AF*, p. 202 (note 29), it is actually from an early draft of *Ecce Homo*.

5 Getting Under the Colonial Skin, Leaping Out of History

1　Related by Francis Jeanson in 'Reconnaissance de Fanon' in the 1965 Seuil edition of *Peau noire*, p. 213.

2　In the original preface to the 1952 Seuil edition of *Peau noire*. See also Jeanson's afterword to the 1965 edition, 'Reconnaissance de Fanon', where he praises Fanon's radical humanism and his intellectual ability to hold everything together (liberatory violence, cultural invention, the transformation of men and of the state).

3　In a study of Fanon's two plays, Keithley Philmore Woolward shows how his re-enactment of the 'underlying "theatricality" of the lived experience of the black man in the context of colonialism' creates the conditions of possibility for its interpretation through 'the discourse of masks and role-playing of the theater event which becomes a form of liberation'. See Keithley Philmore Woolward, 'Towards a Performative Theory of Liberation: Theatre, Theatricality and "Play" in the work of Frantz Fanon', PhD thesis, New York University, 2008, p. 19.

4　Stuart Hall, 'Why Fanon?' [1996], in Hall, *Selected Writings on Race and Difference*, ed. Paul Gilroy and Ruth Wilson Gilmore, ebook (Durham, NC, 2021), pp. 339–57 (343).

6 Socialtherapy: The Breakthrough of Saint-Alban

1　See Camille Robcis, 'Frantz Fanon, Institutional Psychotherapy, and the Decolonization of Psychiatry', *Journal of the History of Ideas*, LXXXI/2 (2020), pp. 303–25 (310–15).

2 See, for example, Frantz Fanon and François Tosquelles, 'Indications de la thérapeutique de Bini dans le cadre des thérapeutiques institutionnelles' (1953) (*AF* 291–8).

3 Marcel Manville, *Les Antilles sans fard* (Paris, 1992), p. 243.

4 For a strong counter-argument, see T. Denean Sharpley-Whiting, 'Anti-Black Femininity and Mixed-Race Identity: Engaging Fanon to Reread Capécia', in *Fanon: A Critical Reader*, ed. Lewis R. Gordon, T. Denean Sharpley-Whiting and Renée T. White (Oxford and Malden, MA, 1996), pp. 155–62.

5 According to Jeanne-Marie Manuellan in her memoir, *Sous la dictée de Fanon* (Paris, 2017).

6 'Interview with Josie Fanon', in Christian Filostrat, *The Last Day of Frantz Fanon: A One-Act Narrative*, ebook (Lake Oswego, OR, 2017), location 646 (of 663).

7 Félix F. Germain, *Decolonizing the Republic: African and Caribbean Migrants in Postwar Paris, 1946–1974* (East Lansing, MI, 2016), p. 90. The substance of these claims is corroborated by the Guadeloupe-born French writer Maryse Condé, who personally knew members of the Fanon family.

8 Julietta Singh, *Unthinking Mastery: Dehumanism and Decolonial Entanglements* (Durham, NC, 2018), p. 29.

9 See Alice Cherki, *Frantz Fanon, portrait* (Paris, 2000), p. 39.

7 Blida: Where Medicine Meets War

1 Frantz Fanon 'Considérations ethnopsychiatriques' (1955) (*AF* 405–9).

2 The paper was subsequently published as 'Conduites d'aveu en Afrique du Nord' (1955) in the conference proceedings (see *AF* 409–12).

3 See Frantz Fanon and Jacques Azoulay, 'La Socialthérapie dans un service d'hommes musulmans: difficultés méthodologiques' (1954) (*AF* 353–72).

4 See Frantz Fanon, François Sanchez and Jacques Azoulay, 'Introduction aux troubles de la sexualité chez le Nord-Africain' (1955) (*AF* 385–94), and Frantz Fanon and Jacques Azoulay, 'La Vie quotidienne dans les douars' (1954–5) (*AF* 373–84).

5 Chaulet performed secret operations on FLN fighters and sheltered the FLN leader Abane Ramdane. Eventually his cover was blown and he was expelled to France.

6 *AF* 198. See Frantz Fanon and Slimane Asselah, 'Le Phénomène de l'agitation en milieu psychiatrique: considérations générales, signification psychopathologique' (1957) (*AF* 437–48).
7 Cited in Joby Fanon, *Frantz Fanon: De la Martinique à l'Algérie et à l'Afrique* (Paris, 2004), pp. 167–9.
8 Alice Cherki, *Frantz Fanon, portrait* (Paris, 2000), p. 93.

8 Public Acts of Provocation: Fanon in Performance

1 A further measure of Fanon's relative outsider status is that he had written to Wright requesting details of his other books but received no response. Fanon would later write about Wright for *El Moudjahid* following his death in 1960.
2 See 'Frantz FANON, Racisme et Culture', www.youtube.com, accessed 1 March 2022. The speech is included in *Pour la révolution africaine* (*PRA* 39–52, *TAR* 31–44).
3 In *Présence africaine*, vol. VIII–X (1956), pp. 193–207.
4 See Alice Cherki, 'Fanon, Fifty Years Later: Resisting the Air of Our Present Time', in *Living Fanon: Global Perspectives*, ed. Nigel C. Gibson (Basingstoke, 2011), pp. 131–8 (134–6).
5 See 'Frantz Fanon, Racisme et Culture' at 00:24:20. Compare with *PRA* 47, *TAR* 39.
6 Cited by Francis Jeanson in his preface to *Peau noire*. See Frantz Fanon, *Peau noire, masques blancs* (Paris, 1965), p. 12. English translation is by David Macey, *Frantz Fanon: A Biography*, ebook (London, 2012), p. 156.
7 Ibid.
8 Ibid.
9 Jeff Sacks, 'Fanon's Insurgence', *Postcolonial Studies*, XXIV/2 (2021), pp. 234–50.

9 My Name is Ibrahim: Exile in Tunis

1 See David Macey, *Frantz Fanon: A Biography*, ebook (London, 2012), p. 300.
2 'Conférence de presse, 4 mai, Tunis', *Le Monde*, 5 June 1957.
3 Frantz Fanon and Charles Geronimi, 'L'Hospitalisation de jour en psychiatrie: valeur et limites. Deuxième partie: considérations doctrinales' (1959) (*AF* 495–512 (499)).

4   See Marie-Jeanne Manuellan, *Sous la dictée de Fanon* (Paris, 2017),
    for her lively account of working with Fanon.
5   See Frantz Fanon, 'L'Hospitalisation de jour en psychiatrie, valeur et
    limites' (1959) (*AF* 473–94), and Fanon and Geronimi, 'L'Hospitalisation
    de jour en psychiatrie'.
6   See 'First Tests using Injectable Meprobamate for Hypochondriac
    States' (*AF* 465–72) for Fanon and Lévy's detailed observations of the
    trial.
7   Cited in Adam Shatz, 'Where Life Is Seized', *London Review of Books*,
    19 January 2017.
8   See 'The Meeting between Society and Psychiatry' (*AF* 511–30) for the
    enlightening notes taken by Bensalem of Fanon's course on social
    pathology.
9   Joby Fanon, *Frantz Fanon: De la Martinique à l'Algérie et à l'Afrique*
    (Paris, 2004), p. 182.
10 See *J'ai 8 ans* (1961), a documentary short directed by Yann Le
    Masson and Olga Poliakoff featuring graphic images of war drawn
    by nine young boys whom Fanon was treating in a refugee camp in
    Tunisia : www.youtube.com, accessed 13 February 2023. For Fanon,
    the expression of visual memories helped traumatized children to
    articulate their splintered understanding of colonial violence.

10 Lifting the Veil/Preaching Revolution

1   Cited by Elaine Mokhtefi in *Algiers, Third World Capital: Freedom
    Fighters, Revolutionaries, Black Panthers*, ebook (London, 2018), p. 42.
2   See Alice Cherki, *Frantz Fanon, portrait* (Paris, 2000), pp. 191–200.
3   Fanon's introduction was subsequently restored by Maspero in future
    editions of the book, which was renamed *Sociologie d'une révolution*.
    The 2011 La Découverte edition used here includes this introduction,
    plus an appendix from the 1960 edition entitled 'Pourquoi nous
    employons la violence' (Why We're Using Violence), the text of a
    speech given by Fanon at the Positive Action Conference for Peace and
    Security in Africa, Accra, April 1960.
4   Nigel C. Gibson, 'The Oxygen of the Revolution: Gendered Gaps and
    Radical Mutations in Frantz Fanon's *A Dying Colonialism*', *Philosophia
    Africana*, IV/2 (2001), pp. 47–62.
5   Jean Khalfa, 'My Body, this Skin, this Fire: Fanon on Flesh', *Wasafiri*,
    XX/44 (2005), pp. 42–50 (45–6).

6 Adam Shatz, 'Where Life Is Seized', *London Review of Books*, 19 January 2017.

7 Cited by Shatz, ibid.

11 Accra, Pan-Africanism and the Southern Front

1 See Jean Daniel Bensaïd, '*Les Damnés de la terre* par Frantz Fanon', *L'Express*, 30 November 1961, p. 36.

2 For a vivid account of this key moment, see Susan Williams, *White Malice: The CIA and the Neocolonisation of Africa* (London, 2021), pp. 43–5.

3 See Frantz Fanon, 'Pourquoi nous employons la violence' (*AV* 171–6).

4 For the official French newsreel account of the conference, which briefly shows Fanon but does not identify him, see *Patrice Lumumba, Frantz Fanon, Mohamed Yazid* (1960) at www.youtube.com, accessed 15 March 2022.

5 Fanon later described the sight to Simone de Beauvoir. See Simone de Beauvoir, *La Force des choses*, vol. II, ebook (Paris, 1972), p. 427.

6 See Elaine Mokhtefi, *Algiers, Third World Capital: Freedom Fighters, Revolutionaries, Black Panthers*, ebook (London, 2018), p. 40.

7 Ibid., p. 41.

8 Extracts were later published as 'This Africa to Come', in *Pour la révolution africaine* (*PRA* 197–211, *TAR* 177–89).

9 See Terry Goldie, 'Saint Fanon and "Homosexual Territory"', in *Frantz Fanon: Critical Perspectives*, ed. Anthony C. Alessandrini, ebook (London and New York, 1999), pp. 75–85 (78).

10 Ibid., p. 79.

11 See Françoise Vergès, 'Chains of Madness, Chains of Colonialism: Fanon and Freedom', in *The Fact of Blackness: Frantz Fanon and Visual Representation*, ed. Alan Read (London, 1996), pp. 46–75 (48).

12 See Matthieu Renault, '*Corps à corps*: Frantz Fanon's Erotics of National Liberation', *Journal of French and Francophone Philosophy*, XIX/1 (2011), pp. 49–55 (53).

13 Ibid.

14 This is the assertion of David Macey, informed by his interview with Joby, in *Frantz Fanon: A Biography*, ebook (London, 2012), p. 419.

15 According to Jeanne-Marie Manuellan, *Sous la dictée de Fanon* (Paris, 2017).

16 In early summer 1960 Fanon had sent Maspero a table of contents for the proposed book, covering the war in the Maghreb and the liberation of Africa, wartime psychiatry, violence in Africa, *négritude* and Negro-African civilization, and ethics and revolution in Algeria. The title of Chapter Six, 'Psychology and History', corresponds to a paper Fanon gave at the World Assembly of Youth in Accra that he wished to publish in *Les Temps modernes* (the text remains lost).

17 See Claude Lanzmann, *The Patagonian Hare: A Memoir*, ebook (London, 2012), p. 338.

18 See Fanon's poignant account of Lumumba's betrayal, 'Lumumba's Death: Could We Do Otherwise?' (*PRA* 212–18, *TAR* 177–89), which bemoans the general failure in the Congo to unite ideologically, and ends with the stirring words: 'the fate of all of us is at stake in the Congo' (*PRA* 218, *TAR* 189).

12 Down to the Wire: The Damned Reborn

1 Claude Lanzmann, *The Patagonian Hare: A Memoir*, trans. Frank Wynne, ebook (London, 2012), p. 337.

2 Miguel Mellino, 'The *Langue* of the Damned: Fanon and the Remnants of Europe', *South Atlantic Quarterly*, CXII/1 (2013), pp. 79–89 (84).

3 See Neil Lazarus, 'Disavowing Decolonization: Fanon, Nationalism, and the Problematic of Representation in Current Theories of Colonial Discourse', *Research in African Literatures*, XXIV/4 (1993), pp. 69–98.

4 John E. Drabinski, 'Fanon's Two Memories', *South Atlantic Quarterly*, CXII/1 (2013), pp. 5–22 (9).

5 Ibid., pp. 13–14.

6 Christopher L. Miller, *Theories of Africans: Francophone Literature and Anthropology in Africa* (Chicago, IL, 1990), pp. 58–9.

7 Adam Shatz, 'Where Life Is Seized', *London Review of Books*, 19 January 2017.

8 See Françoise Vergès, 'To Cure and to Free: The Fanonian project of "Decolonized Psychiatry"', in *Fanon: A Critical Reader*, ed. Lewis R. Gordon, T. Denean Sharpley-Whiting and Renée T. White (Oxford and Malden, MA, 1996), pp. 85–99 (95–6).

9 Simone de Beauvoir, *La Force des choses*, vol. II, ebook (Paris, 1972), p. 421.

10 Ibid., p. 427.

11 Ibid., p. 423.

12   Cited in Alice Cherki, *Frantz Fanon, portrait* (Paris, 2000), pp. 232–3.

13   One such exception was Jean Daniel Bensaïd, who praised the book at
     length in '*Les Damnés de la terre* par Frantz Fanon', *L'Express*,
     30 November 1961, p. 36. For a useful overview of the work's reception
     in France, see Brigitte Riéra, 'La réception des *Damnés de la terre* de
     Frantz Fanon. Un encryptage de l'histoire de la décolonisation', in
     La France et l'Algérie en 1962, ed. Pierre-Louis Fort and Christiane
     Chaulet Achour (Paris, 2013), pp. 57–80.

13 The Final Crossing

1   See Frantz Fanon, 'Blood Flows in the Antilles under French
    Domination' (*PRA* 186–8, *TAR* 167–9). Local tensions had boiled over
    in December 1959 and riots broke out following a racially charged
    altercation between two motorists, resulting in three deaths.

2   Cited in Peter Geismar, *Fanon: The Revolutionary as Prophet* (New York,
    1971), p. 185.

3   Cited in David Macey, *Frantz Fanon: A Biography,* ebook (London,
    2012), p. 484.

4   Simone de Beauvoir, *La Force des choses*, vol. II, ebook (Paris, 1972),
    p. 440.

5   The two speeches by Belkacem and Mendejli, together with a chronicle
    describing Fanon's funeral rites, were published in *El Moudjahid*, 88
    (21 December 1961).

6   Joby Fanon, *Frantz Fanon: De la Martinique à l'Algérie et à l'Afrique*
    (Paris, 2004), pp. 216–17.

7   Beauvoir, *La Force des choses*, vol. II, p. 439.

8   *Le Monde* had originally published the story a year before (23–24
    February 1968) under the title: 'Did Fanon die in the arms of the CIA?'

9   Susan Williams, *White Malice: The CIA and the Neocolonisation of Africa*
    (London, 2021), p. 476.

10   Cited in Assia Djebar, *Algerian White*, trans. David Kelley and Marjolijn
     de Jager [1995] (New York, 2003), p. 174.

11   See 'Introduction' to Simone Browne, *Dark Matters: On the Surveillance
     of Blackness* (Durham, NC, 2015).

12   J. Fanon, *Frantz Fanon*, pp. 207–8.

13   Ibid., pp. 206–7.

14   The interview of 8 June 1978 is available as 'Josie Fanon, interview Jean
     L. Dominique', https://repository.duke.edu, accessed 13 February 2023.

15 Assia Djebar, *Algerian White* [1995] (New York, 2003), pp. 175–6.
16 Ibid., pp. 174–6.
17 See the Algerian writer Djilali Khellas's unverified eyewitness account, '1989, l'année où Josie Fanon s'est suicidée', *El Watan*, 5 July 2011.
18 Claude Lanzmann, *The Patagonian Hare: A Memoir*, trans. Frank Wynne, ebook (London, 2012), p. 350. Lanzmann alleges further that Josie had been in an abusive relationship with a severely jealous, high-ranking member of the Algerian Security Forces that had begun during Fanon's long stays in hospital and continued after his death (p. 348).

14 Fanon's After-Lives

1 Peter Geismar, *Fanon: The Revolutionary as Prophet* (New York, 1971), p. 185.
2 Hannah Arendt, *On Violence* (New York, 1970), pp. 67–70.
3 See Andrew M. Daily, '"It is too soon . . . or too late": Frantz Fanon's Legacy in the French Caribbean', *Karib–Nordic Journal for Caribbean Studies*, II/1 (2015), pp. 26–55.
4 See Matthieu Renault, *Frantz Fanon: De l'anticolonialisme à la critique postcoloniale* (Paris, 2011).
5 See Gavin Arnall, *Subterranean Fanon: An Underground Theory of Radical Change* (New York, 2020).
6 We note that in 2012 Olivier attempted to set up a new Association Nationale Frantz-Fanon in Algiers, but that it has still not been officially recognized by the Algerian authorities.
7 Joby was himself exiled from Martinique in 1967 and forbidden by administrative decree from returning to his homeland owing to his involvement with a French separatist movement on the island.
8 Daily, '"It is too soon"', p. 26.
9 Édouard Glissant, 'Structures de groupes et tensions de groupes en Martinique', *ACOMA*, 1 (1971), p. 39.
10 Ibid.
11 See Jean-François Bayart, 'Postcolonial Studies: A Political Invention of Tradition?', *Public Culture*, XXIII/1 (2011), pp. 55–84.
12 See 'Révolution Frantz Fanon', www.radiofrance.fr, accessed 4 April 2022.
13 Henry Louis Gates Jr, 'Critical Fanonism', *Critical Inquiry*, XVII/3 (1991), pp. 457–70 (457).

14 See Anthony C. Alessandrini, *Frantz Fanon and the Future of Cultural Politics: Finding Something Different* (Lanham, MD, 2014).

15 See Nigel C. Gibson, ed., *Fanon Today: Reason and Revolt of the Wretched of the Earth* (Wakefield, Canada, 2021).

16 Cornel West, 'Introduction', in Frantz Fanon, *The Wretched of the Earth* (New York, 2021).

17 See the *Oxford Bibliography* entry on 'Afro-pessimism' by Patrice Douglass, Selamawit D. Terrefe and Frank B. Wilderson III, www.oxfordbibliog raphies.com. See also Frank B. Wilderson III, *Afropessimism* (New York, 2020), a mixture of memoir and theory that illustrates how Black death is necessary for the material and psychic life of the human species.

18 Frank B. Wilderson III, 'The Narcissistic Slave', www. brotherwisedispatch.blogspot.com, June–August 2016, accessed 14 February 2023.

19 Christina Sharpe, *In the Wake: On Blackness and Being* (Durham, NC, 2016).

20 Nahum Dimitri Chandler, *X – The Problem of the Negro as a Problem for Thought* (New York, 2013).

21 Yohann Koshy, 'The last humanist: how Paul Gilroy became the most vital guide to our age of crisis', *The Guardian*, www.theguardian.com, 5 August 2021.

22 Paul Gilroy, *Against Race: Imagining Political Culture Beyond the Color Line* (Cambridge, MA, 2000), pp. 249 and 341.

23 Paul Gilroy, *There Ain't No Black in the Union Jack* [1987] (Routledge, 2013), pp. 127–8.

24 Achille Mbembe, '*On the Postcolony*: A Brief Response to Critics', *Qui Parle*, XV/2 (2005), pp. 1–49 (19).

25 See 'Achille Mbembe, Frantz Fanon and the Politics of Viscerality', https://humanitiesfutures.org, 27 April 2016. The occasion was a keynote address by Mbembe in April 2016 at Duke University for the workshop 'Frantz Fanon, Louis Mars, & New Directions in Comparative Psychiatry', 26–27 April 2016.

26 Achille Mbembe, *Necropolitics*, ebook [2016] (Durham, NC, 2019), location 3554 (of 4846).

27 Ibid., location 3737–84.

28 Simone de Beauvoir, *La Force des choses*, vol. II, ebook (Paris, 1972), pp. 425–6.

29 See Ayo A. Coly, 'Carmen Goes Postcolonial, Carmen Goes Queer: Thinking the Postcolonial as Queer', *Theory and Critique*, LVII/3 (2016), pp. 391–407 (404).

30 See C. L. Quinan, *Hybrid Anxieties: Queering the French-Algerian War and Its Postcolonial Legacies* (Lincoln, NE, 2020), p. 19.

31 See Will Furtado, 'How Frantz Fanon Has Influenced Generations of Queer Artists', https://contemporaryand.com, 22 June 2018.

32 *Frantz Fanon: Black Skin White Mask* (UK/France, 1996), dir. Isaac Julien and Mark Nash, 19 minutes and 30 seconds.

33 Alice Cherki, 'Fanon, Fifty Years Later: Resisting the Air of Our Present Time', in *Living Fanon: Global Perspectives*, ed. Nigel C. Gibson (Basingstoke, 2011), pp. 131–8 (138).

Select Bibliography

Works by Fanon

L'An v de la révolution algérienne [1959] (Paris, 2011) (includes Fanon's
    original 1959 introduction and 'Pourquoi nous employons la violence'
    (1960)). *A Dying Colonialism*, trans. Haakon Chevalier (New York, 1965)
Les Damnés de la terre [1961] (Paris, 2002) (includes the original preface
    by Jean-Paul Sartre, a new preface by Alice Cherki and a postface
    by Mohammed Harbi). *The Wretched of the Earth*, trans. Constance
    Farrington (London, 2001)
The Fanon Reader, ed. Azzedine Haddour (London, 2006)
Frantz Fanon: Alienation and Freedom [2015] (London and New York, 2018),
    ed. Jean Khalfa and Robert J. C. Young, trans. Steven Corcoran (brings
    together for the first time in English previously unavailable and
    unpublished material)
Peau noire, masques blancs (Paris, 1952). *Black Skin, White Masks*, trans.
    Charles Lam Markmann (London, 1986) (includes a foreword,
    'Remembering Fanon', by Homi Bhabha)
Pour la révolution africaine [1964] (Paris, 2001). *Toward the African
    Revolution*, trans. Haakon Chevalier (New York, 1967) (a posthumous
    collection of essays written from 1952 to 1961)

Articles and books on Fanon

Alessandrini, Anthony C., *Frantz Fanon and the Future of Cultural Politics:
    Finding Something Different* (Lexington, KY, 2014)
——, ed., *Frantz Fanon: Critical Perspectives* (London and New York, 1999)
Arnall, Gavin, *Subterranean Fanon: An Underground Theory of Radical Change*
    (New York, 2020)

Boukman, Daniel, *Frantz Fanon: Traces d'une vie exemplaire*
    (Paris, 2016)
Bulhan, Hussein A., *Frantz Fanon and the Psychology of Oppression*
    (New York, 1985)
Cherki, Alice, *Frantz Fanon, portrait* (Paris, 2000)
Ciriez, Frédéric, and Romain Lamy, *Frantz Fanon* (Paris, 2020)
Confiant, Raphaël, *L'Insurrection de l'âme: Frantz Fanon, vie et mort*
    du guerrier-silex (Lamentin, Martinique, 2017)
Ehlen, Patrick, *Frantz Fanon: A Spiritual Biography* (New York, 2001)
Fanon, Joby, *Frantz Fanon: De la Martinique à l'Algérie et à l'Afrique*
    (Paris, 2004). *Frantz Fanon, My Brother: Doctor, Playwright,*
    Revolutionary, trans. Daniel Nethery (Lanham, MD, 2014)
Filostrat, Christian, *The Last Day of Frantz Fanon: A One-Act Narrative*
    (Lake Oswego, OR, 2017) (includes a 1978 interview with Josie Fanon)
Geismar, Peter, *Fanon: The Revolutionary as Prophet* (New York, 1971)
Gibson, Nigel C., *Fanon: The Postcolonial Imagination* (London, 2003)
——, ed., *Fanon Today: Reason and Revolt of the Wretched of the Earth*
    (Wakefield, Canada, 2021)
——, ed., *Living Fanon: Global Perspectives* (Basingstoke, 2011)
——, and Roberto Beneduce, *Frantz Fanon, Psychiatry and Politics*
    (London, 2017)
Gordon, Lewis R., *Fanon and the Crisis of European Man: An Essay on*
    Philosophy and the Human Sciences (New York, 1995)
——, *What Fanon Said: A Philosophical Introduction to His Life and*
    Thought (Johannesburg, 1996)
——, T. Denean Sharpley-Whiting and Renée T. White, eds, *Fanon:*
    A Critical Reader (Oxford and Malden, MA, 1996)
Haddour, Azzedine, *Frantz Fanon, Postcolonialism and the Ethics*
    of Difference (Manchester, 2019)
Hiddleston, Jane, *Frantz Fanon: Literature and Invention* (Oxford, 2022)
Hudis, Peter, *Frantz Fanon, Philosopher of the Barricades* (London, 2015)
Laubscher, Leswin, Derek Hook and Miraj U. Desai, eds, *Fanon,*
    Phenomenology, and Psychology (New York, 2022)
Lee, Christopher, *Frantz Fanon: Toward a Revolutionary Humanism*
    (Johannesburg, 2015)
Macey, David, *Frantz Fanon: A Biography* [2000], new expanded edition
    (London, 2012)
Manuellan, Marie-Jeanne, *Sous la dictée de Fanon* (Paris, 2017)
Marriott, David S., *Whither Fanon? Studies in the Blackness of Being*
    (Stanford, CA, 2018)

Memmi, Albert, 'The Impossible Life of Frantz Fanon', *Massachusetts Review*, XIV/1 (1973), pp. 9–39 (trans. Albert Memmi, Thomas Cassirer and G. Michael Twomey)

Read, Alan, ed., *The Fact of Blackness: Frantz Fanon and Visual Representation* (London, 1996)

Sekyi-Otu, Ato, *Fanon's Dialectic of Experience* (Cambridge, MA, 1996)

Sharpley-Whiting, T. Denean, *Frantz Fanon: Conflicts and Feminisms* (Lanham, MD, 1998)

Shatz, Adam, 'Where Life Is Seized', *London Review of Books*, XXXIX/2 (19 January 2017), pp. 19–27

Silverman, Max, ed., *Frantz Fanon's 'Black Skin, White Masks': New Interdisciplinary Essays* (Manchester, 2005)

Zelig, Leo, *Frantz Fanon: The Militant Philosopher of Third World Revolution* (London, 2016)

Filmography

Fanon: Hier, aujourd'hui/Fanon: Yesterday, Today (France, 2018), dir. Hassan Mezine, www.vimeo.com/ondemand/fanonhieraujourdhui, accessed 13 February 2023

Frantz Fanon: Black Skin White Mask (UK/France, 1996), dir. Isaac Julien and Mark Nash. The 2017 DVD produced by the BFI includes a useful booklet

Frantz Fanon: Mémoire d'asile/Frantz Fanon: Memories from the Asylum (France, 2008), dir. Bachir Ridouh and Abdenour Zahzah

Frantz Fanon: Une vie, un combat, une œuvre/Frantz Fanon: His Life, His Struggle, His Work (Algeria/France/Tunisia, 2001), dir. Cheikh Djemaï

Re-Reading Fanon (UK, 2021), dir. Nasheed Qamar Faruqi, www7.bbk.ac.uk/hiddenpersuaders/documentaries/re-reading-fanon, accessed 13 February 2023

Sur les traces de Frantz Fanon (France/Algeria, 2021), dir. Mehdi Lallaoui

Radiography

'Racisme et Culture', speech delivered by Fanon at the first International Congress of Black Writers and Artists, Paris, 20 September 1956, www.youtube.com, accessed 13 February 2023

'Révolution Fanon', four-part radio series, France Culture, 5–8 April 2021, www.radiofrance.fr/franceculture/podcasts/serie-revolution-fanon, accessed 13 February 2023

Acknowledgements

I would like first to express my warmest thanks to my publisher Michael Leaman, who originally proposed the idea for this book and whose enthusiastic commitment to the project has been a source of inspiration. I am extremely grateful to Alex Ciobanu, assistant to the publisher and picture editor, for his exceptional editorial support and expertise at every stage. It has been a genuine delight to work with editor Amy Salter and her team on the production of the book. The identity of the external reader of the manuscript must necessarily remain unknown, but I record my appreciation of their many insightful comments and suggestions, which proved immensely helpful in preparing the final version. My thanks also to the Institute for Contemporary Publishing Archives (IMEC) in Caen, which houses the Frantz Fanon Archives (in particular to Julie Le Men); and to the School of Humanities at Royal Holloway, University of London, for generously covering the cost of the images.

The book has benefited enormously from conversations with family, friends and colleagues, in particular Professor Vicki Callahan; Dr Fabrizio De Donno; Professor Catherine Grant; Professor Edward J. Hughes; Professor Eric Robertson; Professor Beryl Satter; and Dr Susan Williams, whose tremendous encouragement and practical advice were invaluable. I would like finally to record my deepest gratitude to Dr Jason Gittens for his unwavering love and support. I dedicate this book to him.

Photo Acknowledgements

The author and publishers wish to express their thanks to the sources listed below for illustrative material and/or permission to reproduce it:

© ADAGP, Paris and DACS, London 2023: pp. 68, 178; Alamy Stock Photo: pp. 18 (Pump Park Vintage Photography), 19 (Archive Farms, Inc/ Caribbean Photo Archive), 23 (Tim Gartside), 42 (Granger – Historical Picture Archive), 91 (Photo12), 100 (Associated Press); © Archives Frantz Fanon/IMEC: pp. 88, 108, 114, 117, 123 (*top*), 137, 139, 140, 144, 148; courtesy Association SACPI: pp. 77, 78 (photo Roman Vigouroux), 80; © Éditions du Seuil, 1952, *Points Essais*, 2015: p. 65; © Fonds Frantz Fanon/IMEC: p. 123 (*bottom*); Getty Images: pp. 40 (Michael Ochs Archive), 131 (Keystone-France/Gamma-Keystone); The Museum of African Art – the Veda and Dr Zdravko Pečar Collection, Belgrade: pp. 150, 156; National Archives at College Park, MD: p. 31; © Présence Africaine: p. 104; © Section photo – Algérie Presse Service/IMEC: p. 168; Wikimedia Commons: p. 171 (photo Alain Cantoux, CC BY-SA 3.0).